creative
cakes
anyone can make

jill foster

Creator of the *Write Way to Cake Decorating*™

Thomas Nelson Publishers

Nashville, Tennessee

www.ThomasNelson.com

To the sweetest part of my life,
Nick and Timothy.

Published by Thomas Nelson, Inc., P.O. Box 141000, Nashville, Tennessee 37214.

Thomas Nelson books may be purchased in bulk for educational, business, fund-raising, or sales promotional use. For information, please e-mail SpecialMarkets@ThomasNelson.com.

Library of Congress Cataloging-in-Publication Data

Foster, Jill, 1961–
    Creative cakes anyone can make / Jill Foster.
        p. cm.
    Includes index.
    ISBN 13: 978-1-4016-0312-0
    ISBN 10: 1-4016-0312-2
    1. Cake decorating. I. Title.
TX771.2.F67 2007
641.8'6539—dc22
2006031265

Printed in China
07 08 09 10 11 RRD 6 5 4 3 2 1

contents

preface

loved making this book because cake decorating appeals to so many people. If you're someone wanting to learn how to decorate cakes but can't take months of lessons, this book is for you. If you're a parent wanting to decorate your child's birthday cake and need quick, easy, money-saving ideas, you'll get them here. If you're an avid cake decorator looking for new and innovative ideas, you'll find more than sixty to choose from. If you want to dress up a dessert cake to make it look like it came from an expensive bakery, here's the place. And if you ever looked at other decorating books and wished they were easier, this book and training DVD will make your dreams come true!

Cake decorating doesn't have to take a lot of time or money. That's why I created the Write Way to cake decorating method. It's the learn-in-one-day method for busy, budgetwise people. In just minutes, you'll turn an ordinary cake into something extraordinary.

Cakes bring a special sentiment to life's important moments. From a baby shower, birthday, graduation, wedding, promotion, or anniversary to retirement, a beautiful cake is the centerpiece of the event. Holiday cakes become part of the festive decor. Bringing a cake you've made warms the hearts of those who receive it. Like a greeting card, a decorated cake sends a message of hope, love, and joy.

I loved experimenting with cakes when I was a teenager, and my family endured them all, including the bright green peppermint cake in which I added the entire bottle of mint extract giving it the flavor of toothpaste! After a few mistakes, I found a way to create simple but sensational cakes, and as the years went by, I decorated cakes for friends and family.

In my twenties I worked in various bakeries as a cake decorator. I loved the challenge and thrill of decorating elaborate and creative cakes. Learning the many decorating techniques and tricks of the trade was fantastic, yet it took hundreds of hours and lots of practice.

In my thirties, I left the cake decorating business to begin a career in children's ministry. Yet, as a new mom, I still enjoyed decorating cakes for my children's parties and special events. I even decorated wedding cakes as gifts for friends who were getting married. People always asked me to teach them how to decorate. Knowing they were as busy as I was and didn't have the time or budget to learn other cake decorating methods, I created my own. I call it the Write Way to Cake Decorating method.

The Write Way method uses your instinctive ability to write. If you think of your decorator bag as a pen and the iced cake as your paper, you can decorate the Write Way. It's simple because you're doing something you've been doing since grade school—writing. This book and training DVD will help you every step of the way. Once you learn the Write Way method, you'll be hooked. You'll create gorgeous cakes that will amaze your friends and family. And you'll have fun doing it!

The cakes in this book are designed to take the stress out of hectic party planning. The majority of them take less than twenty minutes to decorate. They're for people who need "quick and easy" with great results, so you'll have more time to enjoy the event with the people you love. You get to make your cake and eat it too!

Creating this book has been about as much fun for me as creating beautiful cakes. However, I couldn't have done it alone. I thank the amazing people who believed in and cheered on my dream: my wonderful parents, Michael and Sylvia Lodato; incredible sisters, Laura and Kathy; steadfast forever friends Renee, Marla, Joan, Craig, and Scott. Big hugs for my production team: Katherine North, Ann Campbell, and Trudy Neve. Thanks for the laughter, love, and long hours together! Sincere thanks to Geoffrey Stone, senior editor of Rutledge Hill Press, for bringing this project to life. He has taught me what it takes to make a quality book with integrity.

Mostly, thanks to my heavenly Father. My prayer is that this book makes life sweet and simple and becomes your favorite way to decorate from now on. Colossians 1:10–14

Sweet Inspirations,
Jill Foster

Tools and Toppings

Before we get started, you'll need a few tools and toppings. Like an artist, a carpenter, or a seamstress, you need a handy tool kit to hold all your essential tools. Once you've collected these items, you will be able to create all the cakes in this book.

Your tool kit can be as simple or elaborate as you want. I recommend a plastic shoebox, tackle box, or craft organizer to keep all your cake decorating supplies in your kitchen, ready to use. Some of the items below you may already have in your home. The rest can be purchased at your local grocery, craft, or discount store. Most of the items pictured in this book were purchased at Wal-Mart and Target.

TOOLS

1. Food Color Paste or Gel
Food coloring for a cake decorator is like the paint an artist uses. There are several different kinds of coloring, such as pastes, gels, or liquids.

> **Jill's Tip:** If you live in a rural area, you can find all your cake needs on the Internet. Go to my Web site, www.writewaycakes.com for a list of suppliers and tool kit suggestions.

These are found in grocery stores, craft stores, specialty stores, or online. The liquid food coloring found in your local grocery store will do, but the color isn't as vibrant and you will have to use a lot of drops. Adding color paste to white frosting produces vibrant colors. Each cake recipe in this book lists the food colors needed, and with blue, red, green, yellow, violet, and pink in your tool kit, you can make every design in the book.

2. FREEZER PLASTIC STORAGE BAGS OR DISPOSABLE PASTRY BAGS

Freezer storage bags work great as decorator bags. Just cut off a small piece of one of the corners and insert a tip. They hold a tip and frosting well and can be stored in the refrigerator for six weeks. Disposable pastry bags are made especially for cake decorators and are very sturdy. You can find them in the cake decorating aisle in your local discount store.

3. DECORATING TIPS

Although professional cake decorators often use twenty or more different tips, in this book we'll use only seven that I consider essential. Each tip has a universal number. If you cannot find the exact number tip, find the one closest to it. Decorator tips can be found in most discount stores or craft stores. I prefer to use the metal tips instead of the plastic tips. They will last you a lifetime and will keep their shape and performance. I recommend these:

#2 – Small writing tip

#4 – Medium writing tip

#16 – Medium star tip

#18 – Small star tip

#21 – Large star tip

#104 – Medium rose tip

#352 – Medium leaf tip

4. METAL STRAIGHT SPATULA

A straightedge metal spatula is essential to a cake decorator. It has multiple uses and will last you a lifetime. You will use it to spread frosting, fill cakes, fill a decorator bag, and smooth your frosting to make a perfect finish. There are many sizes to choose from—I personally use four-inch and six-inch spatulas.

5. TURNTABLE

You don't need to buy an expensive cake-decorating turntable. I use a lazy Susan of the sort used in pantrys and cupboards—they spin well and clean easily with hot soapy water. You can find inexpensive lazy Susans at any discount or kitchen store.

6. SHARP KNIFE, SCISSORS, AND DENTAL FLOSS

These common household items are handy when decorating a cake. Use a small sharp knife to cut pieces of candy or chopsticks. A large knife, like a bread knife, is used to level your cake. Scissors are used in cutting pieces of candy, lifting off roses, and snipping the ends of your decorator bag. Dental floss is great when leveling a larger cake.

7. RULER

When cutting sticks for a tiered cake, it is important to cut them the correct height and the same height. A ruler is also used to measure lines across a cake.

8. BAMBOO STICKS

Many of the cake designs in this book require the use of bamboo sticks. They can be easily cut with a sharp knife or scissors and pierce well into candy and cakes. Bamboo sticks can be found in most grocery stores in the kitchen utensil aisle.

9. CHOPSTICKS

Chopsticks are used to make beautiful roses (see pages 25-26 in Chapter Three) and for stacking tiered cakes. When you order Chinese food, save

Jill's Tip: After using a metal decorator tip, soak it in hot soapy water. Use a cotton swab to get frosting out of the tip. Once clean, allow it to air dry before storing back in your tool kit.

your chopsticks—or purchase them at a grocery store in the Asian food aisle.

10. CAKE PLATES

Every cake needs a place to sit. Find colorful and beautiful cake plates or flat dinner/serving plates to complement your cake. Most of the plates used in this book were inexpensive and easy to find at a local discount store or thrift store. During the holidays, you can find festive plates to add color and charm to your cakes.

11. CAKE BOARDS

Cake boards are needed when making tiered or stacked cakes. Using a cake board to hold your cake allows you to stack it on top of another cake without the cake board showing. When buying cake boards, you want to find one the same size as your cake pan. Cardboard cake boards can be found in the cake decorating aisle of your craft store.

12. CAKE PANS AND BOWLS

Any ovenproof pan or bowl can be used to bake a cake. Most of the cakes in this book require 8-inch pans (and up to 14-inch pans for wedding cakes). Square pans and rectangle pans are also required in other cake designs. A few of the cake designs require an oven-safe mixing bowl or 4- to 6-cup measuring cup. The new silicone cake pans are fine as long as the cake comes out firm and sturdy when cooled. When choosing the cake pan or bowl for a cake design, use the chart on page 10 in Chapter Two to help plan for the number of cake mixes/recipes needed, as well as the approximate serving size of each pan.

TOPPINGS

Along with the colored frosting, each cake design is adorned with toppings that add creativity and color.

1. CANDIES

There is a large variety of candy sold today and multitudes of ways to use it. Throughout the book you'll see many useful ways to use candy—and the best part about colorful candy toppings is they are edible! (See page 165 for a candy glossary.)

2. FLOWERS

Flowers bring beauty to any cake and are especially nice on anniversary, bridal shower, and wedding cakes. If you are unable to find fresh flowers, most discount or craft stores carry silk flowers that look like the real thing. When using fresh flowers, wash them gently so they're free of any possible pesticides. They should be thoroughly dry before being placed on the cake.

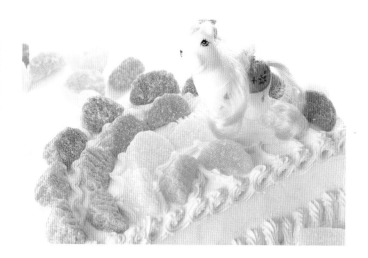

Jill's Tip: Put your fresh flowers on the cake after you have set the cake up where it will be served. Fresh flowers may only look pretty for a while without water; however, you can purchase flower vials at a local florist and insert each stem into a little vial of water.

3. THEME ITEMS

A few of the cake designs in this book require purchasing a decoration to add to the cake. Whether it is a toy pony, a baby bottle, a baby doll, or a stemmed margarita glass to hold a tiered wedding cake, they all complement the cakes. All of the themed decorations used in this book were inexpensive and found at a local discount store.

Next let's take a look at our canvas—a perfect cake—and learn how to prepare the icing.

two

The Right Cake
and Frosting

THE PERFECT CAKE

A well-baked, sturdy cake is the easiest to work with. As a decorator, my goal is to build a moist yet firm cake—and when it's properly baked, cooled, filled, and frosted, a nice, firm cake is a joy to decorate. There are three ways to achieve the perfect cake.

MIXES, HOMEMADE, OR STORE-BOUGHT CAKES

Since my philosophy is all about being simple, quick, and low-cost, I prefer using cake mixes. If the directions on the box are followed correctly, you'll have a wonderful cake to decorate.

> **Jill's Tip:** Cake mixes with pudding in the mix may produce overly moist cakes. Although tasty, I find them to be more difficult to work with when decorating.

If you enjoy baking cakes "from scratch," use a recipe that produces a firm cake. Always use top-quality ingredients, and adequately cool the cake before decorating. I have included some of my favorite cake recipes at the end of this chapter.

When I don't have time to bake a cake, I buy a baked and frosted cake at my local grocery store or bakery. They cost less than the decorated cakes, and I get to decorate the cake my way. Discount club stores have inexpensive half-sheet cakes you can purchase.

PREPARING THE RIGHT CAKE

Here are a few things I've learned about preparing cakes at home, whether from a mix or from scratch:

- Use fresh ingredients in cake mixes or cake recipes. Eggs, butter, and milk need to be new from the grocer.
- Measure ingredients carefully. Unlike cooking, baking requires perfect measuring. My grandmother baked for years, so she knew what a teaspoon of baking soda was in the palm of her hand. I tried that once, and my cake tasted like baking soda! So measure every ingredient just as the recipe calls for. It could mean the difference between a fluffy, moist cake and a dry or flat cake.
- Sift the flour if the recipe calls for it. Cake flour tends to cause lumps, so I always sift it before measuring.

- Add ingredients in the order the recipe indicates. Always add the dry ingredients like flour, salt, baking soda, baking powder, and spices together before adding the wet ingredients.
- Do not overbeat your cake batter. Overmixing makes for an air-filled cake that may bake unevenly. If you think your cake has a lot of air in the batter, tap the cake bowl on the counter—you will see the air bubbles come to the top.
- Grease and dust your cake pans before pouring in the cake batter. First, grease the pan with shortening; then add flour or a small amount of the powdered cake mix to the pan. Shake the pan until all the shortening is coated. You may also use parchment paper to line your cake pans instead of dusting them.

- Preheat the oven before putting a cake in. All recipe baking times are determined from the time you put the cake into the oven at the temperature needed.
- Place cake pans in the center of the oven rack. If two or more pans are used, allow at least an inch of space between the pans and two inches between the pans and the walls of the oven for proper heat circulation.
- No matter how tempted you are to do it, do not open the oven during the first half of the baking time. Just a small amount of cool air can interfere with the rising of the cake.
- Check the cake for doneness before taking it out of the oven. Carefully place a finger on top of the cake and see if the cake bounces back to form. If so, it is done. To be completely sure, you can insert a sharp knife in the middle of the cake. If it comes out clean, the cake is done. If the cake is not done, continue checking every five to ten minutes.

- Cool your cake in the pan at least ten minutes before removing it from the pan. Loosen the cake by sliding a dull knife around the edge of the pan, then turn the cooled cake onto a cake plate or board.
- Cool the cake on the counter for at least one hour. When it reaches room temperature, put it in the refrigerator for a few hours. This will keep the inside of the cake moist and its exterior firm and ready to frost. In fact, I usually bake my cakes the night before an event so there's plenty of time for proper cooling and refrigerating overnight. The next day, I only have to frost and decorate.

NONSTANDARD CAKE SHAPES

Jill's Tip: Large pans—such as the ones you'll need to make tiered cakes—can be found in the cake decorating aisle in discount or craft stores. If you want to save money, see if a friend will let you borrow her set.

Jill's Tip: When making a wedding cake, I do not include the top tier in the serving count. Most wedding couples like to keep their top tier to eat later.

DOME CAKE

A few of the cakes in this book call for using a rounded dome-shaped cake. Use an ovenproof mixing bowl or measuring bowl to create the rounded shape. Grease and flour the bowl before pouring in the cake batter. The dome cakes in this book need only one cake recipe or store-bought mix. Follow the baking instructions as indicated in your recipe or cake mix. To test for doneness, insert a sharp knife to see if the middle of the cake is done. If it is done, the knife will come out clean. If the top of the cake appears done, yet the middle still needs some more baking time, cover the top of the bowl with foil and continue baking until the middle of the cake is done.

RECTANGULAR, SQUARE, OR SHEET CAKE

To create the rectangle or square shapes in many cake designs, you can use a variety of straight-sided cake pans. Most cake pans come in a 13 x 9-inch rectangle or an 8 x 8-inch square. Some cake pans are larger (26 x 18 x 1 or 12 x 18 x 1) and can make a sheet or half sheet cake size. Follow the chart below to determine the amount of cake batter

SERVINGS TABLE		
Pan Size	Number of Recipes/Mixes	Number of Servings
2 (6- or 7-inch) round	1	8
2 (8-inch) round or 2 (8-inch) square	1	10
4-cup mixing bowl (for dome-shaped cake)	1	10
2 (10-inch) round or 1 (13 x 9-inch) rectangle	2	20
2 (12-inch) round or 1 half sheet cake	3	50
2 (14-inch) round or 1 full sheet cake	4	70

needed for each cake. When baking larger size cakes, allow for longer baking times. After thirty minutes in the oven, check every ten minutes for doneness.

ROUND CAKE

Most cakes are round 8-inch or 9-inch cakes. When making wedding or tiered cakes, there is a variety of round pan sizes from which to choose. Use the chart to determine the amount of cake batter for each size cake. After thirty minutes in the oven, continually check every ten minutes for doneness.

PREPARING YOUR PERFECT CAKE FOR DECORATING

If you've baked a cake at home, you'll need to get it ready to be decorated—first by making sure it is level and symmetrical, and then by filling and frosting it. Only then will you be ready to "paint" your masterpiece— the Write Way!

CREATING A LEVEL CAKE

A perfectly formed cake is one where each layer is level. Unless you're using formed pans, a round, square, or rectangular cake needs to be leveled before frosting. Put the cooled and refrigerated cake back into the pan you baked it in. With a long bread knife or string of dental floss, slice across the top of the pan, removing anything above the edge (photo 1). If your baked cake is lower than the height of the pan, you'll just have to do it by eye. Use a bread knife to cut across the top of the cooled cake. Do the best you can to cut a level cake. You will now have a level measurement.

Carefully lift off the top of the cake (photo 2). My children love this part because they get to eat the unused cake!

Now turn the cake over onto a cake plate. You're ready to fill and frost your cake!

5

6

7

Jill's Tip: If I want to create a really smooth finish, I use a blow-dryer on low heat to even out any lines on the cake. I spend the time doing this only with wedding cakes.

FILLING THE CAKE

Most people cut into a cake hoping to find a yummy filling (the part between the layers) to complement the cake. Whether you're using white frosting or fresh strawberries or anything in between, there is a proper way to fill the cake to ensure that it remains level and ready to decorate.

If you're using the same frosting as on the outside of the cake, the process is very easy. With a spatula, smooth frosting evenly over the top of the leveled bottom layer. Place the top layer of cake over the frosting and press gently to connect the frosting to the cake.

If you are filling your cake with another color frosting or type of filling, such as strawberries or mousse, you will need to make a secure border so that the filling does not seep out (photo 3). Prepare a decorator bag (see page 22). Snip a corner of the bag with scissors. Make a border around the edge of the cake by carefully squeezing the frosting out through the snipped corner.

Now you can evenly spread a prepared filling inside the border, using a spatula (photo 4). If you are using a filling that is not spreadable, like fresh strawberries or chocolate chips, spread some frosting first and then arrange your filling ingredients in a single layer on top. Place the second layer on top (photo 5).

FROSTING THE CAKE

The secret to a beautifully frosted cake begins with a great frosting recipe. At the end of this chapter, you'll find frosting recipes I developed and still use on all my cakes. If you use a different recipe for your frosting, make sure it is stiff enough to hold the designs you create. Most store-bought frostings used as is do not hold a design when decorating using the Write Way to Cake Decorating method.

You'll need a prepared batch of frosting, your straight edge spatula, and the turntable. You can store any extra frosting for up to three months in the refrigerator.

Place a filled and leveled cake on the turntable. Frost the sides of the cake first. Using the flat side of the spatula, smooth over the sides without touching the spatula to the cake. Continue adding and pulling the frosting around all the sides (photo 6). Use the turntable to turn the cake as you work the frosting around.

Now pile frosting on top of the cake and evenly smooth it over the top.

With the edge of the spatula, gently glide against the side of the frosting, pulling the spatula toward you as you rotate the cake (photo 7).

Continue guiding the spatula edge as you turn the cake. You may need to add extra frosting if parts of the side are not smoothing well.

If your frosting is too stiff, it may not smooth well; it might even pull crumbs off the cake. If this happens, add small amounts of warm water to make the frosting easier to work with.

If you find the cake is not smoothing well, dip your spatula in hot water, then frost again. Frost the top of the cake the same way. Keep the spatula edge parallel to the cake plate so your cake's top remains level.

KEEPING THE CAKE PLATE CLEAN

To keep a cake plate free of frosting, lay strips of waxed paper around the edges of the plate. Place the cake on top of the plate with the waxed paper strips under the cake. Frost the cake. When finished, carefully slide the strips out from under the cake. Or you can use a paper towel to carefully clean the plate before decorating.

STACKING A TIERED CAKE

Some designs in the following chapters may call for a tiered cake. For a tiered cake you'll need chopsticks (or wooden sticks such as dowels or bamboo sticks) for each layer, a sharp knife, and cake boards.

For each tiered cake, measure the height of the bottom frosted cake using a wooden stick. Using a pen or Sharpie, mark the stick just above (about ⅛ to ¼ inch) the height of the cake.

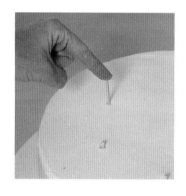

With the sharp knife, carefully cut along the marked line. Cut the stick all the way through or cut halfway and snap in half. Repeat this for three more sticks.

Insert the sticks into the large cake to make a square in the center of the cake. You want to make the square (as shown in the diagram) a good size to hold the next layer, not too large and not too small. For example, if your bottom tier is a 12-inch round cake and you will place a 10-inch round cake on top, you need to place the four sticks toward the center of the cake. This will allow the 10-inch cake to hold and be steady.

Carefully stack the other cake (with cake board underneath) on top of the sticks. If you are taking a tiered cake to another location to serve, assemble the tiers after you arrive at your destination to avoid mishap.

THE RIGHT CAKE RECIPES

Here are three "scratch" recipes that can be used for many memorable cakes! In these and the frosting recipes I use a stand mixer to mix the ingredients. If you have one, it makes the job so much easier. However, if you don't, it is almost as easy to use a handheld electric mixer. Either one will do fine. If you don't have an electric mixer of any kind, be prepared for a mini workout.

YELLOW DREAM CAKE

I love this cake because it's easy to make and so delicious. It creates a sturdy yet moist cake that's perfect for decorating. Makes two 8-inch round cakes.

3	cups sifted all-purpose flour	2	cups granulated sugar
1	tablespoon baking powder	4	large fresh eggs, at room temperature
½	teaspoon salt	1	cup milk, at room temperature
1	cup (2 sticks) butter, at room temperature	1	teaspoon pure vanilla extract

Preheat the oven to 350°F (180°C). Grease the inside of two 8-inch cake pans with shortening and dust with flour. In a large bowl, sift together the flour, baking powder, and salt. In the work bowl of a stand mixer, add the butter and beat on the medium setting for 1 minute (or you can use a mixing bowl and electric beaters). Gradually add the sugar. When needed, stop the mixer to scrape down the sides, making sure all the butter and sugar are well mixed. Beat until light and fluffy. Beat the eggs in a separate bowl and add to the butter mixture. Continue beating until well mixed, scraping down the sides when needed. Turn the mixer to the low setting. Slowly and alternately add the flour mixture and milk. Mix well, then add the vanilla. Spread the batter into the prepared pans about two-thirds high. Smooth evenly. Bake for 25 to 30 minutes. Check for doneness by carefully touching the cake to see if it bounces back. If it is not done, check every 5 minutes.

CHOCOLATE CRAZE CAKE

This delicious cake has a wonderful flavor. I also use this recipe to make chocolate chip muffins—I just add chocolate chips on top of the cupcakes before baking. Yummy! Makes two 8-inch round cakes.

2¼	cups sifted all-purpose flour	¼	teaspoon salt
¾	teaspoon baking soda	2	teaspoons instant coffee granules

½	cup unsweetened cocoa powder	1½	cups granulated sugar
1	cup whole milk	1	teaspoon pure vanilla extract
1½	cups (2½ sticks) butter, at room temperature	3	large fresh eggs, at room temperature

Preheat oven to 350°F (180°C). Grease the inside of two 8-inch cake pans with shortening and dust with flour. In a large bowl, combine the flour, baking soda, salt, coffee, and cocoa powder. In the work bowl of a stand mixer, add the butter and beat on the medium setting for 1 minute (or you can use a mixing bowl and electric beaters). Gradually add the sugar. When needed, stop the mixer to scrape down the sides, making sure all the butter and sugar are mixed well. Beat until light and fluffy then mix in the vanilla. Beat the eggs in a separate bowl. Add the eggs to the butter mixture. Continue beating until well mixed; scrape down the sides when needed. Set the mixer to the low setting. Slowly, alternately add the flour mixture and milk; mix well. Spread the batter into the prepared pans about two-thirds high. Smooth evenly. Bake for 25 to 30 minutes. Check for doneness by carefully touching cake to see if it bounces back. If it is not done, check every 5 minutes.

CARROT SPICE CAKE
This carrot cake is fresh, moist, and fabulous. You must cool and refrigerate it before frosting. Makes two 8-inch round cakes.

2½	cups sifted all-purpose flour	1	teaspoon salt
2	teaspoons baking soda	2	cups granulated sugar
2	teaspoons baking powder	1½	cups vegetable oil
1	tablespoon cinnamon	4	large fresh eggs, at room temperature, beaten
1	teaspoon nutmeg	3	cups shredded carrots
¾	teaspoon cloves		

Preheat the oven to 350°F (180°C). Grease the inside of two 8-inch cake pans with shortening and dust with flour. In a bowl combine the flour, baking soda, baking powder, cinnamon, nutmeg, cloves, and salt. In the work bowl of a stand mixer, combine the sugar and oil and beat on low speed. Add the eggs and beat until the mixture is well mixed. Add the carrots. While on low speed, slowly add the flour mixture. Turn the mixer off to scrape down the sides of the bowl. Mix well but do not overmix. Pour the batter into the prepared pans. Bake for 30 to 35 minutes. Check for doneness by carefully touching the cake to see if it bounces back. If it is not done, check every 5 minutes.

USING CAKE MIXES

As a busy mom, I need quick results, so I regularly use cake mixes to make cakes. Sometimes I like to add ingredients to the mix to give the cake a different flavor. Here are just a few suggestions.

CAKE MIX VARIATIONS

Lemon Zest Cake:

Add 2 tablespoons of lemon zest to a white or yellow cake mix recipe.

Mocha Latte Cake:

Add 1 tablespoon instant coffee granules and ½ cup sour cream to a devil's food cake mix recipe.

Cinnamon Spice Cake:

Add 2 teaspoons cinnamon, ¾ teaspoon nutmeg, and ¼ teaspoon cloves to a yellow cake mix recipe.

Chocolate Chocolate Chip Cake:

Add 1 cup semisweet chocolate chips to a devil's food cake mix recipe.

Chocolate Peanut Butter Cup Cake:

Add ½ cup creamy peanut butter to a devil's food cake mix recipe. Sprinkle 1 cup peanut butter morsels into batter and gently mix.

Chocolate Orange Cake:

Instead of adding the water called for in a chocolate cake mix recipe, add ⅔ cup orange juice and ⅔ cup water. Add 2 tablespoons grated orange zest.

Jill's Tip: You can always refrigerate extra frosting. Put your leftover frosting in a freezer storage bag. Remove the air from the bag and seal well. You can store frosting for up to three months in the refrigerator.

THE RIGHT FROSTING

Making professional decorator's frosting doesn't have to be expensive or difficult. After experimenting with many frosting recipes, I found an easy and quick way to make the frosting you need to decorate any of the cakes in this book. I call it "Wonder Cream" because it is like butter cream without the butter—and it tastes wonderful!

WHITE WONDER CREAM FROSTING

1 tub (16 oz.) store-bought white or vanilla frosting (do not use "whipped" frosting)

1 tub (16 oz.) Crisco shortening (use tub of frosting to measure)

1 pound (16 oz.) box of powdered sugar

¼ cup warm water

Combine the tubs of frosting and shortening into a mixing bowl. On low speed, beat the frosting and shortening until mixed well. While mixer is still on, slowly add the powdered sugar. Add a small amount of warm water until the mixture is smooth. Once all the ingredients are mixed together, beat for about one minute longer. (Do not overmix, as it will leave air bubbles in the frosting, which makes frosting a smooth cake difficult.) If the frosting seems stiff, add some more warm water. If the frosting seems too runny, add powdered sugar.

Note: When making roses, the frosting needs to be very stiff. Add more powdered sugar to get a firm frosting for a beautiful flower that won't droop on the cake.

CHOCOLATE WONDER CREAM FROSTING

1 recipe White Wonder Cream Frosting (page 17)

1 cup unsweetened cocoa powder

¼ cup vegetable oil

Prepare a recipe of White Wonder Cream Frosting. In the work bowl of a stand mixer, whip the cocoa powder and oil together to make a chocolate syrup. Add the syrup to the frosting and beat on low speed for a few minutes. Add additional powdered sugar if needed to make a firmer frosting.

> **Jill's Tip:** I use only Crisco shortening when making frosting. I once used another brand of shortening when making my frosting and it did not create the stiffness and stability needed for decorating.

MOCHA WONDER CREAM FROSTING

1 recipe White Wonder Cream Frosting (page 17)

½ cup instant coffee granules

¼ cup warm water

Prepare a recipe of White Wonder Cream Frosting in the work bowl of a stand mixer. Combine the coffee and water in a mixing bowl and beat together to make coffee syrup. Add to the frosting and beat on low speed for a few minutes. Add additional powdered sugar if needed to make a firmer frosting.

LEMON WONDER CREAM FROSTING

1 recipe White Wonder Cream Frosting (page 17)

4 tablespoons lemon extract

Yellow food coloring paste

Prepare a recipe of White Wonder Cream Frosting in the work bowl of a stand mixer. Add the lemon extract to the frosting while beating on low speed. Add the yellow food coloring a few drops at a time until the desired color is reached. Continue beating for 2 to 3 minutes. Add additional powdered sugar if needed to make a firmer frosting.

Now that you know how to make an appropriate frosting, let's learn how to decorate cakes the Write Way!

Jill's Tip: You may add a teaspoon of any clear extract to give your frosting added flavor. My favorites are vanilla, almond, champagne, lemon, and hazelnut. To find clear extracts that will not discolor your white frosting, go to the cake decorating aisle in discount or craft stores or commercial food stores.

three

The Write Way to
Cake Decorating™ Method

The human brain is an amazing thing. Once you've programmed it by doing something repetitively, you then do that thing automatically—without thinking. Most of what you have programmed into your brain you can do with your eyes closed. If I asked you to close your eyes and tie your shoes, there is a good chance you could do it. Yet recall how many attempts it took to master tying your shoes as a small child; only after practicing over and over did you finally program yourself to tie your shoes without hesitation. That's why other cake decorating methods are difficult to learn; they are teaching you something you have never done before. It takes lots of practice and many hours to learn something new.

In the Write Way to Cake Decorating method, we use what you have been doing since childhood and apply it to cake decorating. Writing comes naturally to people because the letters, numbers, and words are programmed into your brain. If I asked you to write ten *W*'s in a row with your eyes closed, you would have no problem doing that. When asked to sign your name on a document, you don't even have to think about it, you just do it.

The Write Way to Cake Decorating method allows you to create borders and designs by writing letters with frosting. Because you are programmed to write a letter the same way every time, these repetitive letters look like beautiful borders on a cake. When decorating the Write Way, you don't have to think how to write, you just do it. Look at the sequence of vowels and how they can be applied to a cake to create a beautiful border.

aaaaaaa   *eeeeeee*   *iiiiiiiiiii*
ooooooo   *uuuuuuu*

It's that simple! Using the Write Way to Cake Decorating, you repeatedly write the same letter or combination of letters on the cake to create instant borders and designs. Using the A-B-C steps below, you'll be decorating like a pro in just one day.

Note: You can be a sloppy writer and still make creative cakes. As long as you write consistently, your sloppy writing will create a unique and wonderful design.

Try this and you'll see what I mean. Take a pen and paper and without thinking about it, write:

Ten cursive *a*'s in a row
Ten cursive *c*'s in a row
Ten cursive *e*'s in a row
Ten cursive *o*'s in a row

As you see, you consistently created an even-patterned design. On a cake, this makes an evenly spaced border design.

Writing Letters Small, Tight, Extended, or Tall

There are a variety of ways to write the same letter. Small lettering is making your letters small to create smaller designs. Tight lettering is keeping the letters close together as you write. Extended lettering is creating space between each letter as you write in cursive. Tall lettering is writing letters tall and straight.

GET READY TO PRACTICE THE WRITE WAY

Before practicing the Write Way, you need to know how to prepare a decorator bag with frosting. Get out your tool kit and remove a plastic decorator bag or freezer storage bag, decorating tip (use medium star tip for practicing), frosting (see pages 17–18 for frosting recipes), and scissors.

1 Place the decorating tip into the plastic decorator bag, almost any plastic bag will do.

2 Glide the tip to the end of the plastic bag.

3 Using a spatula, fill the bag with frosting.

4 Snip about 2 centimeters off the end (corner) of the bag with scissors, about half the length of the decorating tip.

5 Squeeze the top of the bag slightly to move the frosting down the bag to the tip.

6 Apply pressure to the bag by squeezing gently. Your frosting will flow easily from the tip.

IT'S AS SIMPLE AS A-B-C!

Now that you've prepared a bag of frosting, use the A-B-C steps to make decorating even easier.

A=Apply Pressure

Although you may have a bag full of frosting, do not squeeze from the top. This will create too much pressure and cause uneven writing. Instead, hold the bag a few inches from the tip and apply pressure. Now the frosting will flow smoothly. Use the pointer finger of your nonwriting hand to guide your bag. This helps you keep the bag steady as you write.

B=Bag Position

The angle at which your bag is positioned determines the outcome of the writing on the cake. If you are writing a border of letters on top of the cake, your bag should be tilted toward you as if you were writing on a piece of paper. If you are decorating the side of the cake, your bag should be almost horizontal to the counter. As you practice, you'll find the right bag position that is comfortable and works for you.

C=Consistent Flow

As you decorate, you'll want to be consistent as you write the letters. Always start at the beginning of a letter and continue to write until you need to stop. Always stop at the end of a letter. If needed, turn the cake and begin writing again. Example:

(Start) *cccccccccccc* (End)

READY, SET—PRACTICE!

On a cutting board or upside-down cake pan, practice writing letters using the A-B-C steps.

Look at some of these cakes decorated using the Write Way method to see what you can accomplish using this technique.

In the Spring Garden cake, you see *c*'s on the top border, *w*'s on top of the cake, extended *c*'s on the side of the cake, and *e*'s on the bottom border.

Spring Garden Cake

In the Fish Fun cake, you see *w*'s on the top border, wide *w*'s on the side of the cake, *w*'s on the bottom border, extended *e*'s on the fish body, and small *w*'s on the fish face.

BEYOND BORDERS

There's more than just borders involved in cake decoration. You can create different designs in borders and elsewhere by using different tips for different effects, including size and shape. And don't forget frosting roses and leaves!

Fish Fun Cake

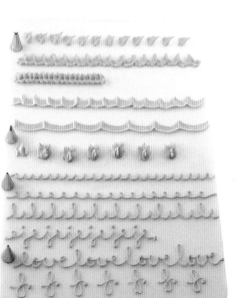

EACH TIP HAS ITS OWN LOOK

As I've noted, there are literally dozens of different tips, and each one creates a different effect. However, the designs in this book use only the seven tips I believe are essential: #2 (small writing tip), #4 (medium writing tip), #16 (medium star tip), #18 (small star tip), #21 (large star tip), #104 (medium rose tip), and #352 (medium leaf tip).

Each decorating tip allows you to make a variety of border designs on a cake.

Star Tips

(from bottom to top) Medium star tip, large star tip designs.

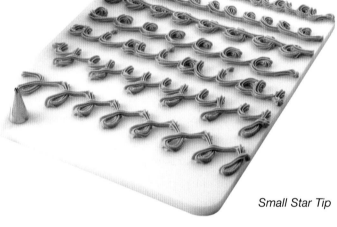

Small Star Tip

Various Tips

(from bottom to top) Medium writing tip, small writing tip, rose tip, and leaf tip designs.

MAKING ROSES THE WRITE WAY

I taught myself how to make roses on a chopstick after delivering a wedding cake on one of the hottest days of the summer—my pretty pink frosting roses had melted as I transported the cake to the reception! With only frosting and a rose tip (I'd left my "rose nail" at home), I went looking for something to use to make replacement roses. The only thing I could find was a chopstick. But in just minutes, there were beautiful roses back on the wedding cake, just in time for the wedding party to arrive. Since then, this has been the only way I make roses!

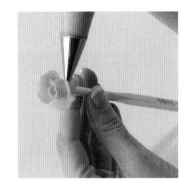

You will need a chopstick, scissors, plastic decorator bag or freezer storage bag, a rose tip, and stiff frosting.

YOUR FIRST ROSE

1. Hold the chopstick between your thumb and first two fingers of your nondominant hand.

2. With a ready-to-use rose tip decorator bag (see *Preparing a Decorating Bag* on page 22), hold the rose tip (skinny side up) parallel to and against the tip of the chopstick and twirl a ring of frosting around the tip of the chopstick. This is the center of the rose.

3. Make three small rose petals around the center by squeezing out three small upside-down *w*'s. Make sure the skinny side of the rose tip is always at the top.

4. Add another layer of larger petals as you turn the chopstick with your fingers.

5. Make roses as small or large as you want. Adding a new row of petals allows the rose to look like a full-blossomed flower.

6. When finished, use opened scissors to lift the rose off the chopstick. Place it carefully on the cake.

NOW ADD LEAVES

Using a leaf tip in a prepared decorator bag, carefully place the tip next to a rose that you've placed on the cake and lift up as you squeeze the bag. Gently pull away until a leaf is formed. Use the leaf tip to make leaves on vines or holly on a Christmas cake (just add red candies) too.

Don't Forget to Add Rosebuds

Rosebuds are tiny roses you make on the cake instead of using the chopstick. To make a single rosebud, using the rose tip make a cursive *i*. To make a larger rosebud, make one rosebud by making a cursive *i*, and two smaller *i*'s to the sides. Add leaves to each rosebud.

YOU'RE READY!

When I design a cake, my goal is that it is easy to make and can be decorated in less than thirty minutes. In fact, most of the cake designs in this book take less than twenty minutes to decorate. As we've discussed, each design you'll see next requires a well-baked, sturdy cake that has been cooled, refrigerated, filled, and frosted. Gather the needed toppings, get out your tool kit, and you are ready to decorate!

> **Jill's Tip:** Make roses ahead of time. Store them on waxed paper in the freezer until ready to use.

Mistakes Can Be Fixed

Mistakes will happen. I have had fingers poked into the cake and things falling on the cake and making designs I didn't want. Here are a few ways to fix mistakes:

1. Use a small sharp knife to lift off any designs or frosting you do not want.
2. Use a spatula to gently spread new frosting over any damaged areas on the cake.
3. Cover mistakes with new frosting designs or lettering.
4. Cover mistakes with candy, flowers, or other decorations.

Thy Word

four

It's a Party!
Birthday Cakes

Jill's Tip: Use colored ice cream cones to make a more colorful cake.

This colorful cake is not only easy but also takes just minutes to decorate. Use this cake for a variety of different occasions, for anyone from a child to an adult—because everyone loves ice cream! Change the frosting color to suit the party décor.

CAKE AND FROSTING

2 (8- to10-inch) round cakes (any flavor), baked, cooled, and refrigerated

2 batches White Wonder Cream Frosting (double the recipe)

TOOLS AND TIPS

Cake plate	Three plastic decorator	Medium star tip
Turntable	bags	Medium writing tip
Metal spatula	Yellow food color paste	Long Knife or
Sharp knife	Blue food color paste	dental floss
Scissors	Large star tip	

Gumballs

3 ice-cream cones

Cake sprinkles

Starburst® colored chewy

  candies, or other

  similar candy

STEP-BY-STEP

1. Remove the cakes from the refrigerator. Level each cake with a long knife or dental floss. Spread White Wonder Cream Frosting or other filling on one of the cakes and place the other cake on top to make a filled cake.

2. Spread White Wonder Cream Frosting over the entire filled cake. Smooth with a spatula.

3. Using a sharp knife, carefully cut down the seam of two ice cream cones. Place the four cone halves on the side of the frosted cake. Cut another cone in half horizontally. Place the top part of the cone in the middle of the cake.

4. Mix about 1 cup of frosting with yellow paste. Continue adding yellow paste until you get the color you want. Repeat this step with blue paste and about 2 cups frosting.

5. Prepare three plastic decorator bags: one with a medium star tip and yellow frosting, the second with a medium writing tip and white frosting, and a third with a large star tip and blue frosting. Clip the ends of the bags with scissors.

6. Using the bag with the medium star tip, write *o*'s around the bottom border of the cake. Make sure the *o*'s are large enough to insert a gumball. Place a gumball inside each *o*.

7. Using the bag with the large star tip, fill the ice cream cones by making *o*'s around the cone. Make a swirl of *o*'s like a soft-serve ice cream cone. Place a red gumball on the top of each cone.

8. Using the bag with the large star tip, make *l*'s on the top border. Then make a single *f* between the cones.

9. Using the medium writing tip, make small gift boxes out of the chewy candies by writing a large plus sign and a cursive capital *J* down the middle, for a bow. Place the gift boxes around the top of the cake. Sprinkle the top of the cake with colorful sprinkles.

The perfect cake for a young girl's dream princess party! Decorate in pinks, yellows, lilac, or all in white for a bridal shower cake. If you need more servings, make the Happily Ever after Castle cake.

CAKE AND FROSTING

1   (6-inch deep) dome cake (any flavor), baked, cooled, and refrigerated
1   batch White Wonder Cream Frosting

TOOLS AND TIPS

Cake plate	Sharp knife	Medium writing tip
Turntable	Two plastic decorator	Rose tip
Metal spatula	bags	
Scissors	Pink food color paste	

TOPPINGS

1 plastic doll

STEP-BY-STEP

1. Place the cooled dome cake on a pretty plate. Using a sharp knife, cut a circle in the top of the cake. Carefully scoop/cut out enough cake to make a hole large enough for the doll to fit. Spread frosting over the entire cake. Smooth with a spatula.

2. Place an undressed doll through the top of the cake with her arms raised.

3. Mix about 1 cup of White Wonder Cream Frosting with pink paste. Continue adding pink paste until you get the color you want. Prepare two plastic decorator bags, one with the medium writing tip and pink frosting and the second with the rose tip and white frosting. Snip the ends of the bags with scissors.

4. Beginning at the top of the doll, make tiny *w*'s around the entire chest and waist of the doll, using the pink decorator bag. Make sure that lowering her arms later won't create a frosting problem. (If you do not want to use frosting to decorate the bodice of the doll, leave the doll's clothes on.)

5. On the top of the cake, make *w*'s around the doll's waist using the white decorator bag. Make sure the wide part of the rose tip is on top when decorating. Continue to make *w*'s around the top part of the cake dome.

6. Using the pink decorator bag, make small *w*'s along the edge of the white *w*'s.

7. Moving down the skirt, continue to make *w*'s around the cake. Add small cursive *ℓ*'s every five *w*'s or so to make a small bow.

8. Finish the bottom border by making *w*'s with the white rose tip.

UNICORN PROMISES

Children will love helping make this cake! And it's so quick and easy you can decorate it in just minutes before the party begins.

CAKE AND FROSTING

1 (8- to 10-inch) round cake (any flavor), baked, cooled, and refrigerated
1 batch White Wonder Cream Frosting

TOOLS AND TIPS

Cake plate	Metal spatula	Yellow food color paste
Turntable	Plastic decorator bag	Medium star tip
Sharp Knife	Scissors	

TOPPINGS

1 large bag of multicolored fruit chews
1 plastic pony or unicorn

1. Cut the cake in half to make a semicircle. Spread frosting on top of one of the cake halves and place the other half on top to create a filled layer cake. Cover the entire cake with White Wonder Cream Frosting and smooth the frosting with a spatula.

2. Mix the rest of the frosting with yellow paste. Continue adding yellow paste until you get the color you want. Prepare a plastic decorator bag with the star tip and yellow frosting. Snip the end of the bag with scissors.

3. Lay red fruit chews along outer edge of the cake to make the first row of the rainbow.

4. With the decorator bag, make extended *w*'s in front of the red fruit chews. Repeat the rows with the orange, yellow, and green fruit chews and extended *w*'s. Make sure you leave room for the pony to be placed on the cake.

5. Place the plastic pony on top of the cake. Push the pony into the cake to secure it.

6. For the top border, using the yellow decorator bag, make *c*'s around the cake. On the bottom border, make tight *l*'s.

This hot rod will come in first place in the hearts of car lovers young and not-so-young!

CAKE AND FROSTING

1 (9 x 13-inch) sheet cake (any flavor), baked, cooled, and refrigerated

2 batches White Wonder Cream Frosting (double recipe)

TOOLS AND TIPS

Rectangular cake plate or white cutting board	Metal spatula	Yellow food color paste
	Sharp knife	Medium star tip
Turntable	Plastic decorator bag	Scissors

> **Jill's Tip:** Change the frosting color to create your car lover's favorite car. Add the number of his favorite NASCAR driver, too!

TOPPINGS

Black licorice twists	Jujy Fruits® candy
Black licorice pieces	Oreo® cookies

STEP-BY-STEP

1. Cut the cake diagonally along the dotted line as shown. Lay one "triangle" on its side and frost the top. Lay the other triangle on

top to create a filled triangle-shaped cake. Cut a small part of the top of the cake to create a ledge (see illustration). Turn the whole thing upright so the right angle is perpendicular to the table.

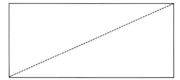 

2. Spread White Wonder Cream Frosting over the entire cake and smooth with a spatula.

3. Mix about 1½ cups frosting with yellow paste. Continue adding yellow paste until you get the color you want. Prepare a plastic decorator bag with the medium star tip and yellow frosting. Snip the end of the bag with scissors.

4. With the star tip, make extended ℓ's along the top and side edges of the cake. Make small 𝒞's along the bottom edge of the cake. Then make 𝒞's along the side of the cake.

5. Place four Oreo cookies around the bottom of the cake to make wheels, two on each side, setting the back wheels one-half inch above the bottom of the cake. Make a large ℴ around the back wheels with yellow frosting.

6. Insert the last Oreo cookie into the center of the cake to make the driver's head. Using yellow frosting, make a helmet on the cookie "face."

7. Finish the hot rod using black licorice and Jujy Fruit candy.

DOTS OF SPRING

This two-tiered spring surprise can be used for many special occasions. Choose a birthday, bridal shower, wedding, anniversary, or spring tea party, and decorate accordingly.

CAKE AND FROSTING

2   (8-inch) round cakes (any flavor), baked, cooled, and refrigerated

2   (12-inch) round cakes (any flavor), baked, cooled, and refrigerated

3   batches White Wonder Cream Frosting (triple recipe)

TOOLS AND TIPS

Large cake plate	Four wood chopsticks	Medium star tip
8-inch cake board	Sharp knife	Long knife or
Turntable	Plastic decorator bag	dental floss
Metal spatula	Yellow food color paste	

TOPPINGS

Necco® Wafers candy

Colorful ribbon gift bow

1. Remove the cakes from the refrigerator. Level each cake with a long knife or dental floss. Spread White Wonder Cream Frosting over one of the leveled 8-inch cakes and place the other 8-inch cake on top. Spread frosting over one of the leveled 12-inch cakes and place the other 12-inch cake on top. Place the larger filled cake on the cake plate and the smaller filled cake on the 8-inch cake board. Spread frosting over both filled cakes and smooth with a spatula.

2. For the lower tier, the 12-inch cake, measure and cut the chopsticks to ⅛ to ¼ inch above the height of the cake. Insert the chopsticks around the center of cake. (See page 13 for complete instructions on stacking a tiered cake.)

3. Carefully place the frosted 8-inch cake onto the chopsticks in the larger cake.

4. Mix about 2 cups frosting with yellow paste. Continue adding yellow paste until you get the color you want. Prepare a plastic decorator bag with the star tip and yellow frosting. Snip the end of the bag with scissors. Make extended *e*'s around the top border. Make wide *w*'s on the bottom tier top border. Then add *y*'s along the side of the top tier, in the middle.

5. Carefully press Necco wafer candies into the sides of both cakes, allowing them to overlap.

6. Top the cake with the ribbon gift bow.

> **Jill's Tip:** In a hurry? Make this cake with one tier—it's just as pretty.

FLOWER SPRAY

Jill's Tip: Make this cake with one or a variety of candy colors.

This simple cake uses my boys' favorite candy—AirHeads. They come in a variety of colors to make effortless flowers and bows. Make this cake for any age birthday or special occasion.

CAKE AND FROSTING

2 (8- to 10-inch) round cakes (any flavor), baked, cooled, and refrigerated
1 batch White Wonder Cream Frosting

TOOLS AND TIPS

Cake plate	Two plastic decorator	Long knife or
Turntable	bags	dental floss
Metal spatula	Large writing tip	Scissors
Green food color paste	Medium star tip	

Jill's Tip: If candy is difficult to work with, heat in the microwave for 3 to 5 seconds to soften.

TOPPINGS

AirHeads® candy (choose a variety of colors)

STEP-BY-STEP

1. Remove the cake from the refrigerator. Level each cake with a long knife or dental floss. Spread White Wonder Cream Frosting or

other filling on one of the cakes and place the other cake on top to make a filled cake. Spread frosting over the filled cake and smooth with spatula.

2. Make seven rosebuds by rolling AirHeads candies tightly in a swirl lengthwise, keeping one end open to make the top of the rosebud. Squeeze the bottom of the rose to make the stem of the flower. Repeat process for six rosebuds. Put the rosebuds on a plate and place them in the freezer until firm and set, about 5 minutes.

3. Make seven bows by folding both sides of the AirHeads candy to the center, then pinching in the middle. Put the bows on a plate and place in the freezer until firm and set, about 5 minutes.

4. Mix 1½ cups frosting with green paste. Continue adding green paste until you get the color you want. Prepare two plastic decorator bags, one with the large writing tip and the second with the medium star tip. Put green frosting in both bags and snip the ends with scissors. Using the bag with the writing tip, make *y*'s along the top border of the cake. Then make extended *l*'s along the side of the cake in the middle. Using the bag with the star tip, make *l*'s and *i*'s along the bottom border.

5. Using the bag with the writing tip, make seven flower stems by creating a curved line along the top of cake.

6. Take the rosebuds and bows out of the freezer and place them on the cake. Place seven rosebuds at the end of each of the stems. Place one bow on top of the cake where all the stems come together and the other six in groups of three on either side of the cake.

This adorable purse will be the girl-talk of the party! Since this cake only serves six to eight people, use the remaining batter to make the quick and easy Flower Bunch cupcakes to serve at the pretty-in-pink party.

CAKE AND FROSTING

1   (8- to 10-inch) round cake (any flavor), baked, cooled, and refrigerated
1   batch White Wonder Cream Frosting

Jill's Tip: Use any pink candies to doll up this cake.

TOOLS AND TIPS

Cake plate	Sharp knife	Plastic decorator bag
Turntable	Scissors	Pink food color paste
Metal spatula	Bamboo sticks	Small star tip

TOPPINGS

Pink licorice twists	Good & Plenty® candy	Pink pillow mints

1. Cut the cake in half vertically. Spread White Wonder Cream Frosting or other filling on top of one of the halves and place the other half on top. Turn the cake upright, on the flat side, and spread frosting over the entire layered cake. Smooth the frosting with a spatula.

2. Mix the rest of the frosting with pink paste. Continue adding pink paste until you get the color you want. Prepare a plastic decorator bag with the small star tip and pink frosting. Snip the end of the bag with scissors.

3. Using the star tip, make a variety of letters across the side of the cake. Make *w*'s, *c*'s, *a*'s, and *ℓ*'s. Make extended *ℓ*'s along the top border and seam of the purse.

4. Place the white Good & Plenty candy and pink pillow mints along the top of the purse.

5. Make the purse handles by using pink licorice twists and bamboo sticks. Snip the ends of licorice and insert a 3-inch piece of bamboo stick on each end. (Bamboo sticks are easily cut with a sharp knife or score with a knife and break off with your fingers.) Repeat the process to make two purse handles.

6. Holding the licorice ends, insert sticks into each side of the purse cake to make a handle.

7. Make the purse bows using 1½-inch pieces of pink licorice. Using scissors, cut along inside of licorice. Open up piece and pinch the middle, creating a small bow (pinch it hard enough so it stays put). Place bows on the side of the purse. Add a small bow tie using the decorator bag with the star tip.

Happy endings are in every little girl's dreams—and this fairy-tale castle cake just might have a Prince Charming waiting inside! Use this cake for any fantasy- or princess-themed party, or make this cake for a bridal shower or to welcome a little girl at a baby shower.

CAKE AND FROSTING

3 (8- to 10-inch) round cakes (any flavor), baked, cooled, and refrigerated

2 batches White Wonder Cream Frosting (double recipe)

Jill's Tip: Use pastel pillow mint candies if you are unable to find mint lentil candies.

TOOLS AND TIPS

Cake plate

Turntable

Metal spatula

Sharp knife

Plastic decorator bag

Pink food color paste

Medium star tip

Scissors

Long knife or dental floss

TOPPINGS

4 sugar ice-cream cones

4 cake ice-cream cones

Heart-shaped candy

Pastel mint lentils

Vanilla and pink wafer
  cookies

STEP-BY-STEP

1. Remove the cakes from the refrigerator. Level each cake with a long knife or dental floss. Spread frosting on top of two of the cakes. Stack them on top of each other and the third cake on top of those. Spread White Wonder Cream Frosting over the entire filled cake. Smooth with a spatula.

2. Using a sharp knife, carefully cut the bottoms off of four cake ice cream cones. Place two of the cone bottoms next to each other on the cake with a little space between them. Stack the other two cone bottoms and place them behind the other cone bottoms to form a triangle.

3. Mix the rest of the frosting with pink paste. Continue adding pink paste until you get the color you want. Prepare a plastic decorator bag with the star tip and pink frosting. Snip the end of the bag with scissors.

4. Make castle turrets by making small *c*'s around a sugar cone. Carefully place the cones on top of the cake cone bottoms already placed on the cake. The last cone will be placed in the middle of the other three "turrets." You should have three levels of turrets. (See photo.)

5. Place wafer cookies on the sides of the cake to make doors and windows to the castle. Using a dab of pink frosting, stick the heart-shaped candy on the doors and windows.

6. Using the star bag, make small *w*'s along the top border and wider *w*'s along the top edge of the cake. Then make *i*'s and *li*'s on the bottom border.

7. Add pastel candies and heart-shaped candies around the cake.

You'll love the sound of this drum! Use it for a child's birthday or to show American pride for military personnel. It can also be used for special holidays like Independence, Memorial, or Veterans Day celebrations. Change the colors to green for the Little Drummer Boy story during the Christmas season. There are so many ways to hear the beat of this drum!

CAKE AND FROSTING

2 (8- to 10-inch) round cakes (any flavor), baked, cooled, and refrigerated
1 batch White Wonder Cream Frosting

TOOLS AND TIPS

Cake plate	Bamboo sticks	Blue food color paste
Turntable	Scissors	Medium star tip
Metal spatula	Plastic decorator bag	Long knife or dental floss

TOPPINGS

Red licorice twists

Fruit streamers, blue and red colors

Red gumballs or Atomic FireBalls®

Two peppermint candy sticks

STEP-BY-STEP

1. Remove the cakes from the refrigerator. Level each cake with a long knife or dental floss. Spread White Wonder Cream Frosting or other filling on one of the cakes and place the other cake on top to make a filled cake. Spread White Wonder Cream Frosting over the filled cake. Smooth with a spatula.

2. Unroll a fruit streamer and wrap it around the bottom of the cake. Using scissors, cut the fruit streamer to fit the cake.

3. Using scissors, cut enough licorice sticks to make *v*'s around the side of the cake. The licorice sticks should be about as long as the cake is tall, and you'll need about 16 cut sticks.

4. Mix the rest of the frosting with blue paste. Continue adding blue paste until you get the color you want. Prepare a plastic decorator bag with a star tip and blue frosting. Snip the end of the bag with scissors. Make small *w*'s in every other triangle along the side of the cake. In the other triangles, edge the red licorice with a line of blue frosting.

5. Make *v*'s along the top edge of the cake. Make wide *w*'s in the center of the cake. Add red gumballs along the top border where the licorice pieces meet.

6. Make a drum handle with 2 licorice twists and bamboo sticks. Snip the ends of the licorice with scissors. Connect the two pieces together with a 1- to 1½-inch piece of bamboo stick. (Bamboo sticks can be easily cut with scissors or score with a sharp knife and snap off with your fingers.) Insert 2-inch pieces of bamboo sticks to each side of the attached handle. Insert the handle into the side of the drum, allowing the handle to rest on the cake plate.

7. Add candy peppermint sticks for drumsticks.

Jill's Tip: If you are unable to find the fruit streamers, decorate the bottom border by making blue frosting *o*'s around the cake. Insert red and blue gumballs inside the *o*'s.

This fancy fish will be the biggest catch at your next beach, luau, summer, or fish fry party. Make it any color using different candy colors.

CAKE AND FROSTING

2 (8- to 10-inch) round cakes (any flavor), baked, cooled, and refrigerated
1 batch White Wonder Cream Frosting

TOOLS AND TIPS

Cake plate	Bamboo sticks	Yellow food color paste
Turntable	Scissors	Medium star tip
Metal spatula	Plastic decorator bag	Long knife or dental floss

TOPPINGS

Fruit chews candy (red, yellow, and orange)	Fruit Roll-ups® M&M's® type candies, or other similar candy	(blue, red, yellow, and orange

1. Remove the cakes from the refrigerator. Level each cake with a long knife or dental floss. Spread White Wonder Cream Frosting or other filling on one of the cakes and place the other cake on top to make a filled cake. Spread White Wonder Cream Frosting over the filled cake. Smooth with a spatula.

2. Mix the rest of the frosting with yellow paste. Continue adding yellow paste until you get the color you want. Prepare a plastic decorator bag with a star tip and yellow frosting. Snip the end of the bag with scissors. Make small *w*'s on the bottom border of the cake.

3. Make fish fins using scissors and fruit chews. Using the scissors, cut the fruit chew candy lengthwise three-quarters of the way down. Carefully fan the fruit chew to make a small fin. Make other fins and press them together, making a large fish fin. Insert at the top and bottom of the cake. Add a red fruit chew for the fish's mouth.

4. Make the fish tail using Fruit Roll-Ups. Cut out seven feather-shaped pieces. For the end of the tail, wrap one Fruit Roll-Ups piece around a 4-inch bamboo stick lengthwise. Continue wrapping the other tail pieces to the bamboo stick to create a flowing tail. Secure the bamboo-stick fish tail into the side of the cake opposite the mouth. Fan out the Fruit Roll-Ups tail so it is open and flowing.

5. Using the yellow decorator bag, make the fish face by making small *w*'s on the right one-quarter of the cake. Place a blue candy for the eye of the fish.

6. Make wide *w*'s along the side and top border with the yellow decorator bag.

7. Make wide *v*'s on top of the cake, separating them with the different colored candies.

Firefighters are special heroes. This fire truck will set off an alarm of happy surprise at any boy's fireman birthday party. Or make this cake to celebrate the firefighter in your life.

CAKE AND FROSTING

2 (13 x 9-inch) cakes (or 1 half sheet cake), baked, cooled, and refrigerated

2 batches White Wonder Cream Frosting (double recipe)

TOOLS AND TIPS

Rectangular cake plate or white cutting board

Turntable

Metal spatula

Bamboo sticks

Scissors

Plastic decorator bag

Medium star tip

Red color paste (or yellow color paste for a yellow fire truck)

TOPPINGS

Red licorice twists

Oreo® cookies

Black licorice twists

Red gumballs or Atomic FireBalls® candy

Red gummy LifeSavers®

Dots® candy

STEP-BY-STEP

1. If using two rectangular cakes, cut each cake to 13 x 6 inches and discard the extra. Frost the top of one cake and place the other cake on top to make one filled cake. If using a half sheet cake, cut it lengthwise into three equal strips. Spread White Wonder Cream Frosting on top of each cake strip and stack all three layers to make a tall, filled cake. If the cake seems unstable, cut 3 or 4 bamboo sticks to the height of the cake and insert to stabilize.

2. Spread White Wonder Cream Frosting over the filled cake and smooth with a spatula.

3. Mix the rest of the frosting with red paste. Continue adding red paste until you get the color you want. Prepare a plastic decorator bag with the medium star tip and red frosting. Snip the end with scissors. Make extended *e*'s along the top of the cake border. Make tight *w*'s along the bottom of the border.

4. Make fire ladders by cutting red licorice twists into equal lengths. Press the "ladder" pieces into the frosting. Make front and side windows, a front grille, and a truck step by cutting equal lengths of black licorice. (See photo for details.)

5. Use red gummy LifeSavers for the front headlights and the end of the fire hose. Make the fire hose by snipping ends of red licorice with scissors. Insert a 1½-inch piece of bamboo stick into both ends of the licorice. Insert one end through a LifeSaver and then into the cake. On the other end, insert a yellow Dot candy. Let the hose rest on the cake plate.

6. Use yellow and red Dots to make lights on the top of the truck.

7. Place Oreo cookies for the wheels. Using a red decorator bag, make tight *o*'s on the Oreo wheels to make hubcaps.

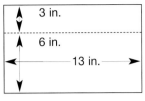

13 x 9-inch
rectangular cake

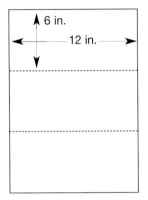

12 x 18-inch
half sheet cake

For the avid gardener, this spring watering can will be a beautiful part of the table décor. Use little flower pots around the cake as party favors and a larger one as a vase to hold flowers to complete the theme.

CAKE AND FROSTING

2   (8-inch) round cakes (any flavor), baked, cooled, and refrigerated

1   batch White Wonder Cream Frosting

TOOLS AND TIPS

Cake plate	Plastic decorator bag	Sharp knife
Turntable	Green food color paste	Long knife or dental floss
Metal spatula	Medium star tip	
Scissors	Bamboo sticks	

TOPPINGS

Chiclets® gum	Green ice cream cake	Pink licorice twists
Mike and Ike® candy	cone	Lemonhead® candies

Jill's Tip: If serving this cake to small children, remove the gum pieces before serving to prevent choking or swallowing the gum.

1. Remove the cakes from the refrigerator. Level each cake with a long knife or dental floss. Spread White Wonder Cream Frosting or other filling on one of the cakes and place the other cake on top to make a filled cake. Spread White Wonder Cream Frosting over the filled cake. Smooth with a spatula.

2. Using a sharp knife, carefully cut an ice cream cone across the bottom at an angle. Gently press the cone into the side of the cake to make a spout.

3. Mix the rest of the frosting with green paste. Continue adding green paste until you get the color you want. Prepare a plastic decorator bag with the medium star tip and green frosting. Snip the end of the bag with scissors. Make *C*'s around the top border of the cake. Make *e*'s around the bottom border and extended *C*'s around the side of the cake.

4. Lay gum pieces on top of the cake in a row just above the ice cream cone. Make a row of *e*'s using a star tip. Repeat this pattern until you have two rows of candies.

5. Follow the instructions on how to make a handle in the Pretty in Pink Purse cake. (See page 41). Make one handle with pink licorice twist. Insert the handle in the side of the cake.

6. Decorate the cake using Mike and Ike candy to make flower petals, and lemon drops for flower centers as in the photo. Place gum pieces and lemon drops around the cake.

FOOTBALL FANATIC

This football field cake will really score at any sports fan's birthday or Super Bowl party. My oldest son Nick's football picture adorns the cake center.

CAKE AND FROSTING

1 (13 x 9-inch) rectangle cake (any flavor), baked, cooled, and refrigerated
2 batches White Wonder Cream Frosting (double recipe)

TOOLS AND TIPS

Rectangular cake plate or white cutting board	Ruler	Medium star tip
	Scissors	Medium writing tip
Turntable	Plastic decorator bag	Long knife or dental floss
Metal spatula	Green food color paste	

Jill's Tip: Instead of a favorite photo, insert a football card of a favorite team or player.

TOPPINGS

Fruit Roll-Ups®	2 Nerds® ropes	4 pretzel sticks
Dots® candy	Green cake sprinkles	
Green sour rope candy	3 x 5 plastic photo frame	

1. Remove the cake from the refrigerator. With a long knife or dental floss, level the cake. Turn the cake onto a cake plate or cake board so the flat side is on top.

2. Spread White Wonder Cream Frosting over the cake. Smooth with a spatula.

3. Using a ruler, mark lines across the cake to make yard lines. With scissors, cut equal lengths of green sour rope and place on the lines. Sprinkle green sprinkles over the field.

4. Place a Nerds rope on both sides of the field to represent people in the stadium. Place Dots candy on the field to represent the football players.

5. Mix the rest of the frosting with green paste. Continue adding green paste until you get the color you want. Prepare a plastic decorator bag with a star tip and green frosting. Snip the end of the bag with scissors. Make *e*'s and small *j*'s around the top border. Make extended *e*'s around the bottom border of the cake.

6. With green frosting, make a swirl in the center of the cake. Place a photo frame on top of the cake in this frosting swirl.

7. Using the scissors, cut two Fruit Roll-Ups seven inches long. Roll a Fruit Roll-Up around the top of a pretzel, pinching gently to hold in place. Wrap the other end of the Roll-Up around the top of another pretzel and pinch to secure.

    Insert the pretzel goalposts into each end of the field.

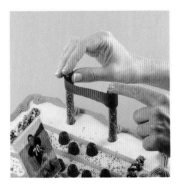

Simple and sweet makes this cake a quick solution for any occasion. Just changing the candy colors and types makes a different look that's appropriate for any age. Have fun with it!

CAKE AND FROSTING

2 (8- to 10-inch) round cakes (any flavor), baked, cooled, and refrigerated

1 batch White Wonder Cream Frosting

TOOLS AND TIPS

Cake plate	Two plastic decorator	Small star tip
Turntable	bags	Styrofoam coffee cup
Metal spatula	Pink food color paste	Long knife or dental floss
Scissors	Medium star tip	

TOPPINGS

Pastel-colored mint lentils

Round sugar cookies

1. Remove the cakes from the refrigerator. Level each cake with a long knife or dental floss. Spread White Wonder Cream Frosting or other filling on one of the cakes and place the other cake on top to make a filled cake. Spread White Wonder Cream Frosting over the filled cake. Smooth with a spatula.

2. Carefully tuck sugar cookies halfway into the cake bottom.

3. Mix some frosting with pink paste. Continue adding pink paste until you get the color you want. Prepare two plastic decorator bags: one with a small star tip and pink frosting, the other with a medium star tip and pink frosting. Snip the ends of the bags with scissors.

4. With a Styrofoam cup, make a half circle on top of the cake on the right edge as shown in photo. Repeat directly across on the left side, then make two more at the top and bottom so that the half-circles are evenly spaced and symmetrical.

5. With the small star tip bag, make small *w*'s around the half-circle pattern on top of the cake. With the medium star tip bag, make *y*'s on the top border and *d*'s on the bottom border.

6. Place candies in a floral pattern around the cake on top and sides. Using dabs of icing, secure the candies to the cookies to make a floral pattern.

This party cake will be all the rage with your guests. The cake is full of surprises with candy party blowers, gumballs, candy streamers, and a candy spray coming out of the cake.

CAKE AND FROSTING

2 (8- to 10-inch) round cakes (any flavor), baked, cooled, and refrigerated
1 batch White Wonder Cream Frosting

TOOLS AND TIPS

Cake plate	Scissors	Blue food color paste
Turntable	Two plastic decorator	Medium star tip
Metal spatula	bags	Small star tip
Bamboo sticks	Yellow food color paste	Long knife or dental floss

> **Jill's Tip:** Reduce decorating time by using only one frosting color, and Fruit Roll-Ups instead of Nerds strips to make party blowers.

TOPPINGS

Fruit Roll-Ups®	Xtreme Nerds® strips	Gumballs
Red licorice twists	Candy sticks (a variety of	
Dots® candy	colors)	

1. Remove the cakes from the refrigerator. Level each cake with a long knife or dental floss. Spread White Wonder Cream Frosting or other filling on one of the cakes and place the other cake on top to make a filled cake. Spread White Wonder Cream Frosting over the filled cake. Smooth with a spatula.

2. Mix 1 cup frosting with blue paste. Continue adding blue paste until you get the color you want. Prepare a plastic decorator bag with the medium star tip and blue frosting. Repeat with 1 cup frosting and yellow paste and the small star tip. Snip the ends of the bags with scissors.

3. Cut a Fruit Roll-Ups lengthwise to make two long strips. Cut four 6-inch strips and wrap around a bamboo stick to make a "streamer." Press tightly so the candy will hold to the bamboo, and place in the freezer for about 5 minutes or until firm.

4. With blue frosting, make one large l (extending to the center of the cake) and two smaller l's around the top of the cake. Repeat three times, dividing the cake into four quadrants. Make a swirl of o's in the center of the cake.

5. Using yellow frosting, make w's along the bottom border and large w's on top of the cake.

6. Press candy sticks around the side of the cake. Add colorful gumballs along the side of the cake.

7. Break a candy stick in half to make a "party blower." On the broken end, attach a rolled up candy strip. Secure the candy with a small strip of Fruit Roll-Ups. Pinch gently to get the candy to stick. Rest each party blower on top of a gumball.

8. When the streamers are firm, gently slide them off the bamboo sticks and place on top of the cake. Place gumballs around the top of the cake.

9. Cut three 8-inch long bamboo sticks and three 6-inch-long licorice twists. Insert a stick into the licorice. Then pierce two Dots candies with the top of the stick. Insert the bottom of the stick into the middle of the cake at a festive angle as shown.

People of all ages love to ride a carousel—the antique horses, pretty lights, and carnival music put a smile on anyone's face. Light the candles and relive your carousel memories!

CAKE AND FROSTING

2   (8- to 10-inch) round cakes (any flavor), baked, cooled, and refrigerated
1   batch White Wonder Cream Frosting

TOOLS AND TIPS

Cake plate	Bamboo sticks	Blue food color paste
Turntable	Scissors	Medium star tip
Metal spatula	Plastic decorator bag	Long knife or dental floss

TOPPINGS

Candles	Frosted circus animal	Pixy Stix®
Red licorice twists	cookies (pick out the	Gumballs
Gummy LifeSavers®	camels to use as	
Dots® candy	carousel horses)	

1. Remove the cakes from the refrigerator. Level each cake with a long knife or dental floss. Spread White Wonder Cream Frosting or other filling on one of the cakes and place the other cake on top to make a filled cake. Spread White Wonder Cream Frosting over the filled cake. Smooth with a spatula.

2. Mix the rest of the frosting with blue paste. Continue adding blue paste until you get the color you want. Prepare a plastic decorator bag with a medium star tip and blue frosting. Snip the end of the bag with scissors.

3. With blue frosting, make extended *w*'s around the top border of the cake. Repeat the *w*'s on top of the cake, mirroring the *w*'s you already made. Make *v*'s around the bottom border of the cake, large enough to allow a gumball to be inserted in the middle.

4. Press Pixy Stix into the sides of the cake at the point of the *w*'s to represent the horse poles. Press a frosted camel cookie over the Pixy Stix.

5. Insert gumballs around inside the *v*'s on the bottom border. With blue frosting, make a single *z* in between each horse and pole.

6. With scissors, cut six 6-inch long licorice twists and one 5-inch-long piece. With a sharp knife or scissors, cut seven 7-inch-long pieces of bamboo sticks. Insert the sticks through the licorice pieces. Push two Dots candies and one gummy LifeSaver into a 5-inch licorice stick. Insert the stick into the center of the cake. One by one, insert one end of the 6-inch licorice twists into the cake and the other end into a Dots candy that is on the center "pole."

7. Insert candles through the gummy LifeSavers and stick them into the cake top between the licorice sticks.

Jill's Tip: Have a friend help you create the carousel "roof" by holding the licorice twists as you insert another one. It makes assembling easier.

ISLAND FANTASY

Your island dreams are just minutes away with this trouble-free seascape cake. Perfect for a beach bash, luau, summer birthday, or retirement celebration.

CAKE AND FROSTING

2 (8- to 10-inch) round cakes (any flavor), baked, cooled, and refrigerated
1 batch White Wonder Cream Frosting

TOOLS AND TIPS

Cake plate	Sharp knife	Blue food color paste
Turntable	Scissors	Medium star tip
Metal spatula	Plastic decorator bag	Long knife or dental floss

TOPPINGS

Gummy fish and sea life candy	Dots® candy	Drink umbrellas (optional)
Swedish Fish®	Green fruit chews or candy mint leaves	

Jill's Tip: When filling the cake, press gummy fish into the frosting before adding the top layer for a surprise when guests dive into the cake!

1. Remove the cakes from the refrigerator. Level each cake with a long knife or dental floss. Spread White Wonder Cream Frosting or other filling on one of the cakes and place the other cake on top to make a filled cake. Spread White Wonder Cream Frosting over the filled cake. Smooth with a spatula.

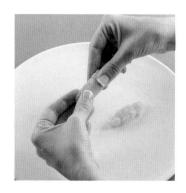

2. Mix the rest of the frosting with blue paste. Continue adding blue paste until you get the color you want. Prepare a plastic decorator bag with a medium star tip and blue frosting. Snip the end with scissors. Make extended *C*'s around the side and bottom border of the cake to make waves. Press Swedish Fish and gummy sea life to the sides of the cake.

3. With your fingers, flatten the green fruit chews to make palm leaves. With scissors, cut the edges of the candy to fan the leaves.

4. With a knife, cut yellow Dots candy in half lengthwise to make a palm tree trunk. Cut the tops of the candy to make coconuts. Place trunk pieces in a curve on top of the cake. Lay down the palm branches, and place coconut candy pieces on top of the leaves.

5. With blue frosting, make *C*'s around the top border and the lower half of the cake top for the ocean.

6. With a knife, cut Dots candy pieces in half lengthwise to make flower petals. Arrange the petals to form island flowers on top of the cake. Cut yellow Dots candy tops to make flower centers.

7. Stick some drink umbrellas in the cake for added festiveness, if desired.

TURTLE-RIFIC!

This adorable green turtle may be too cute to eat! It's so easy you can make many of them to line a tabletop for your party.

CAKE AND FROSTING

1   dome cake (any flavor), baked, cooled, and refrigerated
1   batch White Wonder Cream Frosting

TOOLS AND TIPS

Cake plate	Plastic decorator bag	Medium star tip
Turntable	Scissors	Long knife or dental floss
Metal spatula	Green food color paste	

TOPPINGS

Hostess Cupcakes®	Jujy Fruits® candy
Large green gumdrops	Dots® candy

STEP-BY-STEP

1. Spread White Wonder Cream Frosting or other filling over the cooled cake. Smooth with a spatula.

2. Cut two cupcakes in half and place on the sides of the dome for turtle legs. Put another cupcake in the front for the turtle head. Spread a thin layer of white frosting over the cupcakes.

3. Mix the rest of the frosting with green paste until you get the color green you want. Fill a plastic decorator bag with a medium star tip and green frosting. Snip the end with scissors.

4. With green frosting, make *n*'s around the turtle's legs and a large swirl of *o*'s for the turtle's head. Press black Jujy Fruits into the bottom of the legs of the turtle to make toes. Press two black Jujy Fruit candies into the face for eyes and one red one for a nose.

5. On the body of the turtle, using the green frosting, make swirl of *o*'s all around.

6. Using your fingers, create a dozen or so pieces of "shell" by pressing a yellow Jujy Fruit candy into a large gumdrop. Arrange these around the body of the turtle spaced alternately in two rows. Create a third row of just yellow Jujy Fruit candies between the shell pieces.

7. On top of the body, make *w*'s around in circles. Insert one yellow Jujy Fruit candy on top in the middle of the shell.

Balloons, party hats, and teddy bears adorn this bright colored cake—
just the thing to make a toddler giggle with joy!

CAKE AND FROSTING

2 (8- to 10-inch) round cakes (any flavor), baked, cooled, and refrigerated
1 batch White Wonder Cream Frosting

TOOLS AND TIPS

Cake plate	Scissors	Medium star tip
Turntable	Plastic decorator bag	Long knife or dental floss
Metal spatula	Blue food color paste	

TOPPINGS

Ice-cream sugar cones	Gumballs	Red licorice string
Cinnamon bears	Fruit Jewels or large	
Red Hots® candy	gumdrops	

STEP-BY-STEP

1. Remove the cakes from the refrigerator. Level each cake with a long knife or dental floss. Spread White Wonder Cream Frosting or other filling on one of the cakes and place the other cake on top to make a filled cake. Spread White Wonder Cream Frosting over the filled cake. Smooth with a spatula.

2. Mix the rest of the frosting with blue paste. Continue adding blue paste until you get the color you want. Prepare a plastic decorator bag with a medium star tip and blue frosting. Snip the end of the bag with scissors. Make *l*'s around the bottom border of the cake. Make *w*'s around the top border.

3. With scissors, cut six 5-inch long licorice strings.

4. With your fingers, flatten six gumdrops to look like balloons.

5. Carefully, press bears into the bottom border. Press a licorice string behind a bear and bring it up and over the top border of the cake. Press a candy balloon on top of the licorice string. Place another string and bear near the first. Place two more pair of bears and balloons around the cake, leaving room for a cone between each pair.

6. Carefully "cut" one-third of three of the cones lengthwise by using your fingers. Carefully break the pieces from the sugar cones to give a ragged edge to one side. Be sure to leave the pointy part intact. This will allow you to press them easily into the side of the cake. Press three of the cones to the side of the cake between each pair of bears and balloons. With blue frosting, make *w*'s around the cone to make party hats. Add Red Hots and gumballs around the party hat.

7. With blue frosting, make *w*'s around the fourth ice-cream cone. Place it in the center of the cake. Add Red Hots and gumballs around the party hat on top of the cake.

FLOWER BUNCH

These single-serving cupcakes are a great favorite. They're cute and colorful, and everyone gets a lollipop and candy too. A wonderful treat to bring to your child's classroom or a brunch or buffet, they're so easy to make—you can whip up a batch for dessert tonight!

CAKE AND FROSTING

12 to 24 cupcakes (any flavor), cooled

1 batch White Wonder Cream Frosting

TOOLS AND TIPS

Cake plate	Pink or blue	Medium writing tip
Two plastic decorator	food color paste	Scissors
bags	Medium star tip	

TOPPINGS

Dum Dum Pops®

Mike and Ike® candy, tropical flavor

STEP-BY-STEP

1. Prepare a decorator bag with the star tip and White Wonder Cream Frosting. Snip the end of the bag with scissors. Make a swirl of *o*'s on top of a cupcake.
2. Mix the rest of the frosting with pink or blue paste. Continue adding paste until you get the color you want. Prepare a second decorator bag with the writing tip and pink or blue frosting. Snip the end of the bag with scissors.
3. Make rounded *l*'s around the cupcake to make flower petals.

4. Press one end of the colorful Mike and Ike candies in each petal, allowing the candy to stick up to represent a blooming flower.
5. Insert an unwrapped lollipop in the center of each cupcake.

Caution: Dum Dum Pops can be a choking hazard for very small children if not properly supervised.

Hallmark
Holiday Cakes

When the clock strikes midnight, it's time to celebrate with bubbly and cake! This timely ticker will ring in the New Year sweetly.

CAKE AND FROSTING

2 (8- to 10-inch) round cakes (any flavor), baked, cooled, and refrigerated

1 batch White Wonder Cream Frosting

TOOLS AND TIPS

Cake plate

Turntable

Metal spatula

Scissors

Bamboo sticks

Small 4-inch plate or
   circle pattern

Two plastic decorator
   bags

Blue food color paste

Medium star tip

Medium writing tip

Long knife or dental floss

TOPPINGS

AirHeads® candy, variety of colors

1. Remove the cakes from the refrigerator. Level each cake with a long knife or dental floss. Spread White Wonder Cream Frosting or other filling on one of the cakes and place the other cake on top to make a filled cake. Spread White Wonder Cream Frosting over the filled cake. Smooth with a spatula.

2. Using a small plate or circle pattern, make a circle outline in the center of the cake.

3. Mix the rest of the frosting with blue paste. Continue adding blue paste until you get the color you want. Prepare a decorator bag with a writing tip and blue frosting. Snip the end of the bag with scissors. Prepare a second bag with a star tip and blue frosting.

4. With the writing tip make small *w*'s around the center circle to make the outer edge of the clock. Write the numbers 12, 3, 6, and 9 around the clock. Write the clock hands by making two arrows.

5. Make candy streamers using AirHeads candy. With scissors, cut three strips lengthwise. Wrap each strip gently around a bamboo stick. (See how-to photos on page 113.)

    Put the wrapped bamboo sticks in the freezer until firm, about 5 minutes. Once they're firm, remove them from the freezer and gently slide off the bamboo sticks. Lay the candy streamers around the clock.

There's nothing sweeter on Valentine's Day than a heart-filled cake. Surprise that someone you love the most with this pretty cake!

CAKE AND FROSTING

2 (8- to 10-inch) round cakes (any flavor), baked, cooled, and refrigerated
1 batch White Wonder Cream Frosting

TOOLS AND TIPS

Cake plate	Scissors	Medium star tip
Turntable	Plastic decorator bag	Heart cookie cutter
Metal spatula	Pink food color paste	Long knife or dental floss

TOPPINGS

Red Hots® candy	Candy hearts

1. Remove the cakes from the refrigerator. Level each cake with a long knife or dental floss. Spread White Wonder Cream Frosting or other filling on one of the cakes and place the other cake on top to make a filled cake. Spread White Wonder Cream Frosting over the filled cake. Smooth with a spatula.

2. Use a heart cookie cutter to make a heart pattern in the center of the cake.

3. Mix the rest of the frosting with pink paste. Continue adding pink paste until you get the color you want. Prepare a decorator bag with the medium star tip and pink frosting. Snip the end of the bag with scissors.

4. With pink frosting, make small *o*'s around the edge of the heart. Make small *c*'s in the inside edge of the heart. Place Red Hots around the heart.

5. Make *j*'s around the top border around the cake.

6. Write *l-o-v-e* around the top border. Write one *l* and three *w*'s continuously around the bottom border.

7. Decorate the cake with candy hearts and Red Hots.

Bunnies, bunnies everywhere! Children are filled with wonder during the Easter season with all the bunnies, chicks, eggs, and jellybeans.

CAKE AND FROSTING

2 (8- to 10-inch) round cakes (any flavor), baked, cooled, and refrigerated
1 batch White Wonder Cream Frosting

TOOLS AND TIPS

Cake plate	Plastic decorator bag	Scissors
Turntable	Yellow food color paste	Long knife or dental floss
Metal spatula	Medium star tip	

TOPPINGS

Plastic eggs	PEEPS® bunnies
Green sour rope	Small jelly beans

1. Remove the cakes from the refrigerator. Level each cake with a long knife or dental floss. Spread White Wonder Cream Frosting or other filling on one of the cakes and place the other cake on top to make a filled cake. Spread White Wonder Cream Frosting over the filled cake. Smooth with a spatula.

2. With scissors, cut equal lengths of sour rope and place around the sides of the cake to form vertical stripes. Place about 1½ inches apart.

3. Cut varying lengths (½ to 1 inch) of sour rope to make Easter grass. Layer the pieces around the top of the cake.

4. Mix the rest of the frosting with yellow paste. Continue adding yellow paste until you get the color you want. Prepare a decorator bag with the star tip and yellow frosting. Snip the end of the bag with scissors. Make v's down the sides of the cake in every other stripe. Make extended ℓ's around the top border.

5. Open five plastic eggs and place on the cake. Fill one-half of the eggs with a dab of frosting. Place Peeps bunnies inside the eggs. Sprinkle the top of the cake with jelly beans.

> **Jill's Tip:** Hide jelly beans in the filling to add a colorful surprise.

Moms will cherish this lovely teapot, a memento of special times spent with special women friends. Make this cake for a church brunch, a women's luncheon, or a little girl's tea party. I used my grandmother's old-fashioned china plate to serve this teapot.

CAKE AND FROSTING

2   dome cakes (any flavor), baked, cooled, and refrigerated.

1   batch White Wonder Cream Frosting

TOOLS AND TIPS

Cake plate	Scissors	Long knife or dental floss
Turntable	Plastic decorator bag	Sharp knife
Metal spatula	Pink food color paste	
Bamboo sticks	Medium writing tip	

TOPPINGS

Blue and white AirHeads® candy

Pink licorice twists

STEP-BY-STEP

1. Remove the cakes from the refrigerator. Cut just the top off one of the dome cakes using a long knife or dental floss so it can sit upside

down without tipping. Turn the cake upside down and spread White Wonder Cream Frosting over the flat side of the cake. Place the other dome cake on top right side up. Spread White Wonder Cream Frosting over the entire cake. Smooth with a spatula.

2. Make two white rosebuds from AirHeads to adorn the bottom of the cake. Make rosebuds by rolling AirHeads candies tightly in a swirl lengthwise, keeping one end open to make the top of the rosebud. Squeeze the bottom of the rose to make the stem of the flower. Repeat the process and place the rosebuds on a plate and put in the freezer until firm and set, about 10 minutes. (See Flower Spray cake how-to photos on page 39.)

3. Mix the rest of the frosting with pink paste. Continue adding pink paste until you get the color you want. Prepare a decorator bag with a writing tip and pink frosting. Snip the end of the bag with scissors. Make a variety of letters around the teapot. Make *W*'s, *l*'s, and *C*'s.

4. Flatten a blue AirHeads candy and form it into a circle. Place it over the top of the teapot to make a lid. Then roll another blue AirHeads candy to make a ball. Put the ball in the refrigerator to cool and firm, about 10 minutes.

5. With scissors, cut three strips of blue AirHeads candy lengthwise. Wrap the strips around the base of the teapot, trimming them to fit.

6. To make a teapot handle, snip the ends of licorice and insert a 3-inch piece of bamboo stick on each end. (Bamboo sticks are easily cut with a sharp knife or scoring with a knife and breaking off with your fingers.) Insert the bamboo stick into the side of the teapot. (See the how-to illustration on the Pretty in Pink Purse cake on page 41.)

7. To make the spout, cut three 3-inch pieces of licorice with scissors. Then cut three 5-inch bamboo stick pieces. Insert the sticks into the licorice.

8. Flatten a blue AirHeads candy and place the three licorice pieces on top. Roll the AirHeads candy over the licorice and pinch at the ends.

9. Insert the teapot spout into the side of the cake opposite the handle.

10. Remove the rosebuds and candy ball from the freezer. Attach the candy ball to the top of the lid with a little pink frosting. Arrange the rosebuds around the base of the cake.

Mother's Day is a day to thank our moms for all they do for us—and this charming hat will touch any mother's heart. You can also make this hat for other special occasions such as women's events, a bridal shower, or even a Kentucky Derby brunch.

CAKE AND FROSTING

1   dome cake (any flavor), cooled and refrigerated

1   (8- to 10-inch) round cake (any flavor), baked, cooled, and refrigerated

1   batch White Wonder Cream Frosting

TOOLS AND TIPS

Cake plate	Scissors	Long knife or dental floss
Turntable	Plastic decorator bag	
Metal spatula	Medium star tip	

TOPPINGS

Mike and Ike® candy, tropical flavor

Red AirHeads® candy

1. Spread White Wonder Cream Frosting over the entire cake. Smooth with a spatula.

2. Prepare a decorator bag with a star tip and white frosting. Snip the end of the bag with scissors. Make *w*'s around the base of the dome cake and *c*'s around the bottom of the cake.

3. Decorate around the cake with Mike and Ike candies to make flowers.

4. With scissors, cut red AirHeads candy into two strips. Fold each strip over and pinch together. Put the ends together and wrap with another 1½-inch strip to form the bow. Open the bow with your fingers.

5. Cut two 3-inch strips to make the ribbons flowing from the bow. Pinch the ribbon to the back of the bow. Place the bow on the back of the hat.

FISHING WITH DAD

Children of all ages love to go fishing with Dad or Grandpa. This easy-to-make cake is a reminder of those special times—and will be the big catch of Dad's special day.

CAKE AND FROSTING

2 (8- to 10-inch) round cakes (any flavor), baked, cooled, and refrigerated
1 batch White Wonder Cream Frosting

TOOLS AND TIPS

Cake plate	Plastic decorator bag	Scissors
Turntable	Blue food color paste	Long knife or dental floss
Metal spatula	Medium star tip	

TOPPINGS

Pretzel rods or candy sticks	Gummy fish and frogs Swedish Fish®	Red licorice strings

1. Remove the cakes from the refrigerator. Level each cake with a long knife or dental floss. Spread White Wonder Cream Frosting or other filling on one of the cakes and place the other cake on top to make a filled cake. Spread White Wonder Cream Frosting over the filled cake. Smooth with a spatula.

2. Mix 1 cup frosting with blue paste. Continue adding blue paste until you get the color you want. Prepare a decorator bag with a star tip and blue frosting. Snip the end of the bag with scissors. Make C's around the bottom border of the cake. Make C's across half of the cake to make the ocean. Make swirls to create a small frog pond on top of the cake.

3. Tie a licorice string to a pretzel rod. Stick one pretzel rod out of the top of the cake and attach the string to a Swedish fish. Make another pretzel rod and string to stick to the side of the cake, attaching the string to another fish.

4. Decorate the cake with candy fish and frogs.

Celebrate American pride on Independence Day with this red, white, and blue flag. Make this flag for any military event, Veterans Day, Memorial Day, or even a political event.

CAKE AND FROSTING

1 (9 x 13-inch) rectangular cake (any flavor), baked, cooled, and refrigerated
1 batch White Wonder Cream Frosting

TOOLS AND TIPS

Cake plate or
   white cutting board
Turntable
Metal spatula
Scissors

Bamboo sticks
Two plastic decorator
   bags
Blue food color paste
Medium star tip

Small star tip
Small star cookie cutter
Long knife or dental floss

TOPPINGS

Red licorice twists
Blue and red AirHeads® candy

1. Remove the cake from the refrigerator. With a long knife or dental floss, level the cake. Cut the cake lengthwise to make two 9 x 6 ½-inch cakes. Spread White Wonder Cream Frosting over the top of one of the cakes and smooth with a spatula. Place the other cake on top to make a filled rectangular cake. Spread White Wonder Cream Frosting over the filled cake. Smooth with a spatula.

2. With scissors, cut three strips of red AirHeads candy lengthwise. Wrap the strips around the bamboo sticks to make streamers. (See the how-to illustration in Way to Go! cake on page 113.) Place the wrapped strips in the freezer until firm, about 5 minutes.

3. With scissors, cut the licorice twists to an appropriate length to form the stripes of the flag.

4. Mix 1 cup frosting with blue paste. Continue adding blue paste until you get the color you want. Prepare a decorator bag with a small tip and blue frosting. Snip the end of the bag with scissors. Make *v*'s in the upper corner of the flag.

5. Prepare a decorator bag with a medium star tip and white frosting. Snip the end of the bag with scissors. Make *v*'s along the edge of the licorice stripes.

6. With the white frosting bag, make small stars inside each blue *v*.

7. Flatten blue AirHeads candy and make stars with the cookie cutter. Stick the stars to the sides and top of the cake.

8. When they're firm, slide the streamers off the sticks and place them around the edges of the cake for decoration.

COFFEE BREAK

Everyone deserves a break from the daily grind of work! This coffee mug cake is a fun excuse to enjoy a cup of java with your closest friends.

CAKE AND FROSTING

3 (8- to 10-inch) round cakes (any flavor), baked, cooled, and refrigerated
1 batch White Wonder Cream Frosting
1 batch Mocha Wonder Cream Frosting

TOOLS AND TIPS

Cake plate	Three plastic decorator	Scissors
Turntable	bags	Foil
Metal spatula	Small star tip	Long knife or dental floss
Bamboo sticks	Medium star tip	
Green food color paste	Medium writing tip	

Jill's Tip: Custom design your coffee mug by changing the frosting color and candies.

TOPPINGS

1 large (5 oz.) dark chocolate bar	Brown and green M&M's® type candies, or other	Red or black licorice twists
Rolled wafer cookies	similar candy	

1. Heat the oven to 350 degrees.

2. Remove the cakes from the refrigerator. Level each cake with a long knife or dental floss. Spread Mocha Wonder Cream Frosting or other filling on top of two of the cakes. Stack them on top of each other and place the unfrosted cake on top to make a filled three-layer cake.

3. Spread White Wonder Cream Frosting over the entire cake. Smooth with a spatula.

4. Line an 8-inch round cake pan with foil. Break pieces of the chocolate bar into the pan. Heat the chocolate for 8 to 10 minutes in the oven. Take the pan of melted chocolate out of the oven and cool on a wire rack, about 10 minutes. Once cool, put the pan of chocolate in the refrigerator until firm, about 10 minutes. When firm, take the foil out of the pan and carefully peel off the chocolate. With the textured side up (the wrinkled texture looks more like coffee), lay the chocolate over the top of the cake.

5. Mix ½ cup frosting with green paste. Continue adding green paste until you get the color you want. Prepare a decorator bag with a writing tip and green frosting. Snip the end of the bag with scissors. Make 𝓎's around the top side of the cake and 𝓌's around the center side of the cake.

6. Fill a decorator bag with the medium star tip and Mocha Wonder Cream Frosting. Snip the end with scissors. Make fancy 𝒸's in between 𝓎's.

7. Prepare a decorator bag with the small star tip and White Wonder Cream Frosting. Snip the end of the bag with scissors. Make 𝓵's around the bottom border. On the top of the chocolate, make a swirl of 𝑜's to represent whipped cream. Place two rolled wafer cookies in the "whipped cream."

8. With the white frosting bag, make 𝒿's around the top border, touching the edge of the chocolate.

9. Make coffee mug handles using bamboo sticks and licorice twists. Follow the handle instructions for the Pretty in Pink Purse cake on page 41 Once assembled, insert the handles into the side of the mug.

10. Decorate the coffee mug with the brown and green candies.

This creepy-crawly cake will keep your guests spinning. So simple to make, you'll have plenty of time to get your costume on. Trick or Treat!

CAKE AND FROSTING

2 (8- to 10-inch) round cakes (any flavor), baked, cooled, and refrigerated

1 batch White Wonder Cream Frosting

TOOLS AND TIPS

Cake plate	Plastic decorator bag	Medium writing tip
Turntable	Green food color paste	Scissors
Metal spatula	Long knife or dental floss	

TOPPINGS

Black licorice twists	Tube of black frosting	Large black gumdrops

STEP-BY-STEP

1. Remove the cakes from the refrigerator. Level each cake with a long knife or dental floss. Spread White Wonder Cream Frosting or other filling on one of the cakes and place the other cake on top to

make a filled cake. Spread White Wonder Cream Frosting over the filled cake. Smooth with a spatula.

2. Mix $\frac{1}{2}$ cup frosting with green paste. Continue adding green paste until you get the color you want. Prepare a decorator bag with a writing tip and green frosting. Snip the end of the bag with scissors. Make a dot in the upper top of the cake. This will be your starting point to making the spider's web. From this point, make long, straight lines across and down the cake. Make *w*'s connecting to each line on the top of the cake.

3. With a tube of black frosting, make a large swirl of *o*'s near the center of the web to make the body of the large spider. Place a large gumdrop on top of the black frosting *o*. Make a face with the green frosting.

4. Press other large gumdrops around the cake to represent climbing spiders.

5. Make spider legs by cutting long strips of licorice twists lengthwise. Cut eight equal 1-inch lengths for each smaller spider. Make the legs of the large spider $1\frac{1}{2}$ inches long.

Jill's Tip: Add more to this cake by decorating with candy pumpkins and candy corn.

Everyone will fall in love with this festive cake. Celebrate the changing of colors and the autumn harvest with this pumpkin patch cake.

CAKE AND FROSTING

2 (8- to 10-inch) round cakes (any flavor), baked, cooled, and refrigerated
1 batch White Wonder Cream Frosting

TOOLS AND TIPS

Cake plate	Sharp knife	Medium star tip
Turntable	Plastic decorator bag	Scissors
Metal spatula	Green food color paste	Long knife or dental floss

TOPPINGS

Orange and green fruit chews	Candy corn
	Large orange gumdrops

1. Remove the cakes from the refrigerator. Level each cake with a long knife or dental floss. Spread White Wonder Cream Frosting or other filling on one of the cakes and place the other cake on top to make a filled cake. Spread White Wonder Cream Frosting over the filled cake. Smooth with a spatula.

2. Using a sharp knife, sliver off the sides of orange fruit chews to create sticky sides. You will need ten fruit chews to make a large pumpkin. Connect the orange slices to make a large pumpkin. Gently squeeze the pumpkin to make sure all the slices are sticking together. Place the pumpkin in the center of the cake.

3. Using a knife, cut down the side of the green fruit chews to make pumpkin leaves. Position the leaves around the center pumpkin and the small leaves on top of the pumpkin.

4. With your fingers, squeeze orange gumdrops to form a pumpkin shape. Place them around the top of the cake's edge. Add green leaves and candy corn.

5. Mix the rest of the frosting with green paste. Continue adding green paste until you get the color you want. Prepare a decorator bag with the medium star tip and green frosting. Snip the end of the bag with scissors. Make *v*'s around the bottom border of the cake. Make *x*'s around the top border.

6. Using a knife, cut orange gumdrops and green fruit chews in half. Press them into the cake around the bottom border, alternating between orange gumdrop, green fruit chew, and candy corn. Add a dot of green frosting to the top of each pumpkin around the bottom border.

The month of November has an air of thankfulness as we contemplate all our blessings of the past year. This cornucopia cake is overflowing with a bountiful harvest.

CAKE AND FROSTING

2 (8 or 10-inch) round cakes (any flavor), baked, cooled, and refrigerated
1 batch White Wonder Cream Frosting

Jill's Tip: Instead of using white frosting to make your borders, make green, yellow or orange frosting. To make orange frosting, mix red and yellow food paste with white frosting.

TOOLS AND TIPS

Cake plate	Plastic decorator bag	Small autumn leaf cookie
Turntable	Medium star tip	cutter
Metal spatula	Scissors	Long knife or dental floss

TOPPINGS

Ice-cream sugar cone	Light and dark green
Fruit-shaped candy	AirHeads® candy

1. Remove the cakes from the refrigerator. Level each cake with a long knife or dental floss. Spread White Wonder Cream Frosting or other filling on one of the cakes and place the other cake on top to make a filled cake. Spread White Wonder Cream Frosting over the filled cake. Smooth with a spatula.

2. Prepare a decorator bag with a star tip and white frosting. Snip the end of the bag with scissors. Make *C*'s around the bottom border of the cake. Make *y*'s around the top border.

3. Using your fingers, carefully break pieces from the sugar cones to give a ragged edge to one side. Be sure to leave the pointy part intact. This will allow you to press it easily into the top of the cake on its side. Place candy fruit flowing out of the cone and around the side of the cone. Place a few fruit pieces around the bottom border.

4. Flatten the AirHeads candies and, using the leaf-shaped cookie cutter, make small leaves. Shape the leaves with your fingers until they bend slightly to look more like falling leaves. Place the leaves around the top of the cake.

Jill's Tip: To soften AirHeads candy, put them in the microwave for 3 to 5 seconds. This makes it easier to mold and flatten them.

This tree-lined cake is the perfect centerpiece for a holiday party. It's so easy to make, it could be a special Christmas baking project with your children.

CAKE AND FROSTING

2 (8- to 10-inch) round cakes (any flavor), baked, cooled, and refrigerated
1 batch White Wonder Cream Frosting

TOOLS AND TIPS

Cake plate   Plastic decorator bag   Medium star tip
Turntable   Scissors   Long knife or dental floss
Metal spatula   Green food color paste

TOPPINGS

Ice-cream sugar cones	Peppermint sticks or
Red Hots® candy	candy canes

STEP-BY-STEP

1. Remove the cakes from the refrigerator. Level each cake with a long knife or dental floss. Spread White Wonder Cream Frosting or other filling on one of the cakes and place the other cake on top to make a filled cake. Spread White Wonder Cream Frosting over the filled cake. Smooth with a spatula.

2. Mix the rest of the frosting with green paste until you get a vibrant Christmas green color. Prepare a decorator bag with the medium star tip and green frosting. Snip the end of the bag with scissors.

3. Make *j*'s around the top border of the cake. Repeat making *j*'s over the top of the first ones for the look of a Christmas wreath.

4. Using your fingers, carefully break pieces from eight sugar cones to give a ragged edge to one side. Be sure to leave the pointy part intact. This will allow you to press them easily into the side of the cake.

5. Place another cone upside down in the top center of the cake.

6. With green frosting, make *c*'s around the bottom border of the cake. Then add small *w*'s around each sugar cone. Decorate with Red Hots candies.

7. With green frosting, make single *j*'s on the sides of the cake between every other set of trees. Make six *j*'s on the top of the cake around the center tree. Decorate with Red Hots.

8. Place peppermint sticks or candy canes on the sides of the cake between the trees.

Shower Power Cakes

This delightful baby carriage will bring smiles to any baby shower. Change the frosting color to pink if you know it's a girl or green if it's still a secret.

CAKE AND FROSTING

2 (8- to 10-inch) round cakes (any flavor), baked, cooled, and refrigerated
1 batch White Wonder Cream Frosting

TOOLS AND TIPS

Cake plate	Two plastic decorator	Medium star tip
Turntable	bags	Scissors
Metal spatula	Blue food color paste	Long knife or dental floss
Sharp knife	Large star tip	

TOPPINGS

Round sugar cookies
Pastel pillow mints

1. Remove the cakes from the refrigerator. Level each cake with a long knife or dental floss. Spread White Wonder Cream Frosting or other filling on one of the cakes and place the other cake on top to make a filled cake. Spread White Wonder Cream Frosting over the filled cake. Smooth with a spatula.

2. Mix 2 cups frosting with blue paste. Continue adding blue paste until you get the color you want. Prepare a decorator bag with a medium star tip and blue frosting. Snip the end of the bag with scissors. Make *C*'s around three-quarters of the side of the cake, leaving a small area that will be the carriage opening. Make *C*'s around three-quarters of the top border, to match. Outline the carriage opening (like a pie shape) for the baby's head (see photo).

3. Fill the carriage shape in by making *C*'s across the top of the cake. A one-quarter pie shape will be left white.

4. To make wheels, prepare a decorator bag with a large star tip and white frosting. Snip the end of the bag with scissors. Make a large *&* around a sugar cookie. Stack another cookie on top. Continue this process with four cookies. Make two wheels.

5. With blue frosting, make a tire and a hubcap for each wheel by making a large *&* around the edge of the top cookie and a smaller *&* in the center of the top cookie.

6. With a sharp knife, cut one biscuit cookie to make a baby's face (one-quarter pie shape). Place the cookie in the stroller (see photo). With blue frosting, make the face, head, and hair.

7. Decorate the cake with pillow mints.

This charming baby bib is perfect for a new mom's baby shower. You can create this cake in just minutes, so there's time to look pretty for the party.

CAKE AND FROSTING

2   (8- to 10-inch) round cakes (any flavor), baked, cooled, and refrigerated
1   batch White Wonder Cream Frosting

TOOLS AND TIPS

Cake plate	Plastic decorator bag	Styrofoam coffee cup
Turntable	Yellow food color paste	Scissors
Metal spatula	Medium star tip	Long knife or dental floss

TOPPINGS

Pastel pillow mints	Baby bottle candy (take
Pink licorice twist	the wrapper off)

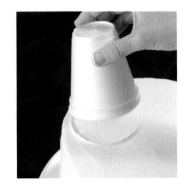

1. Remove the cakes from the refrigerator. Level each cake with a long knife or dental floss. Spread White Wonder Cream Frosting or other filling on one of the cakes and place the other cake on top to make a filled cake. Spread White Wonder Cream Frosting over the filled cake. Smooth with a spatula.

2. Using a Styrofoam coffee cup, make a ring on top of the cake to create the neck opening of the bib.

3. Mix the rest of the frosting with yellow paste. Continue adding yellow paste until you get the color you want. Prepare a decorator bag with a medium star tip and yellow frosting. Snip the end of the bag with scissors.

4. Make *e*'s and *c*'s continuously around the bottom border. Make *c*'s around the top border. Make extended *e*'s inside the bib to give it a design. Then make small *c*'s around the neck of the bib, following the circle you created with the Styrofoam cup.

5. With scissors, cut two equal lengths of licorice. Place at the tie of the neck.

6. Decorate the cake with pillow mints and the baby bottle.

Jill's Tip: Change the frosting color to blue or pink if you know the baby is a boy or girl.

This wonderful baby shower cake will be the perfect centerpiece for your decorated table. You can even use the cake as a game to play with guests: just count how many candies you put in the baby bottle and ask everyone to guess the number. The person closest wins the bottle of candy or other prize!

CAKE AND FROSTING

2 (8- to 10-inch) round cakes (any flavor), baked, cooled, and refrigerated
1 batch White Wonder Cream Frosting

TOOLS AND TIPS

Cake plate	Plastic decorator bag	Styrofoam coffee cup
Turntable	Blue food color paste	Scissors
Metal spatula	Medium star tip	Long knife or dental floss

TOPPINGS

Plastic baby bottle	Candy-coated almonds	Candy to fill baby bottle

STEP-BY-STEP

1. Remove the cakes from the refrigerator. Level each cake with a long knife or dental floss. Spread White Wonder Cream Frosting or other filling on one of the cakes and place the other cake on top to make a filled cake. Spread White Wonder Cream Frosting over the filled cake. Smooth with a spatula.

2. Using a Styrofoam cup, make half-circle markings around the top of the cake, as shown in photo.

3. Mix the rest of the frosting with blue paste. Continue adding blue paste until you get the color you want. Prepare a decorator bag with a medium star tip and blue frosting. Snip the end of the bag with scissors. Make *w*'s along the half-circle markings.

4. Make *j*'s around the top border and *l*'s around the bottom border. Make single *s*'s on the side of the cake.

5. Place a candy-filled baby bottle in the center of the cake. Decorate around the bottle and the bottom of the cake with candy almonds.

Watching a baby sleep is one of the precious times of parenting. The mom-to-be will adore this sweet lullaby cake. It looks very difficult to make, yet it's quite easy (but that will be our secret).

CAKE AND FROSTING

2 (8- to 10-inch) round cakes (any flavor), baked, cooled, and refrigerated
1 batch White Wonder Cream Frosting

TOOLS AND TIPS

Cake plate	Pink or blue food color	Waxed or parchment
Turntable	paste	paper
Metal spatula	Small star tip	Long knife or dental floss
Plastic decorator bag	Scissors	

TOPPINGS

Baby doll (small enough to lay on the cake)
Pastel mint lentils or pillow mints

1. Remove the cakes from the refrigerator. Level each cake with a long knife or dental floss. Spread White Wonder Cream Frosting or other filling on one of the cakes and place the other cake on top to make a filled cake. Spread White Wonder Cream Frosting over the filled cake. Smooth with a spatula.

2. Mix 1½ frosting with pink or blue paste. Continue adding pink or blue paste until you get the color you want. Prepare a decorator bag with a star tip and pink or blue frosting. Snip the end of the bag with scissors.

3. Make a pillow by outlining a small rectangle and filling it in with small *w*'s.

4. Lay the undressed baby doll on top of the pillow with the baby's face turned to the side.

5. Cut a large square of waxed or parchment paper. Fold it in half diagonally to make a triangle large enough to cover the entire baby.

6. Spread frosting evenly over the paper triangle, going over the edges. Smooth with a spatula. Carefully lift the paper triangle and lay it over the baby.

7. With pink or blue frosting, make extended *e*'s along the edge of the baby blanket. Make a wide row of *w*'s across the baby blanket. Next, place a row of candies across the blanket. Repeat with the *w*'s and the candies until the whole blanket is decorated.

8. With pink or blue frosting, write *u* continuously around the bottom border. Decorate with pastel candies.

This precious quilt allows you to make a variety of cute pattern blocks. Its pink and blue design is perfect if no one knows whether the coming baby is a boy or girl.

CAKE AND FROSTING

1   (9 x 13-inch) rectangle cake (any flavor), baked, cooled, and refrigerated
1   batch White Wonder Cream Frosting

TOOLS AND TIPS

Cake plate or white
   cutting board
Turntable
Metal spatula
Scissors

Two plastic decorator
   bags
Pink food color paste
Blue food color paste
Small star tip

Medium star tip
Ruler
Long knife or dental floss

TOPPINGS

Baby decoration for top of cake

STEP-BY-STEP

1. Remove the cake from the refrigerator. Turn the cake over onto the cake plate or board. Spread White Wonder Cream Frosting over the cake. Smooth with a spatula.

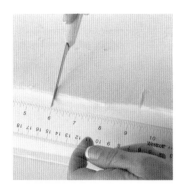

2. Mix white frosting with pink paste. Continue adding pink paste until you get the color you want. Prepare a decorator bag with a small star tip and pink frosting. Snip the end of the bag with scissors. Repeat using blue paste and a medium star tip.

3. Using a ruler, measure four 3¼-inch sections on the long side of the cake. Use a ruler to score lines across the cake. Repeat by measuring three 3-inch lines on the short side and scoring lengthwise. This will create twelve quilt blocks.

4. With blue frosting, trace the lines separating the blocks. Using both pink and blue frosting, make a variety of designs in the blocks using letters, shapes, and lines. Have fun thinking of ways to make interesting patterns!

5. Make *u*'s continuously around the bottom border. Make single *v*'s along the side of the cake.

6. Top the cake with a cute baby decoration.

Delicate and pretty is the theme of this bridal shower or anniversary cake. Adorning it with a few fresh flowers brings a dainty charm to the finished cake.

CAKE AND FROSTING

2 (8- to 10-inch) round cakes (any flavor), baked, cooled, and refrigerated

1 batch White Wonder Cream Frosting

TOOLS AND TIPS

Cake plate	Small writing tip	Scissors
Turntable	Two plastic decorator	Long knife or dental floss
Metal spatula	bags	
Small star tip	Styrofoam coffee cup	

TOPPINGS

Fresh flowers

1. Remove the cakes from the refrigerator. Level each cake with a long knife or dental floss. Spread White Wonder Cream Frosting or other filling on one of the cakes and place the other cake on top to make a filled cake.

2. Spread White Wonder Cream Frosting over the filled cake. Smooth with a spatula.

3. Mix ¾ frosting with 2 teaspoons warm water to thin the frosting. It needs to flow easily without being runny. Prepare a decorator bag with a writing tip and white frosting. Snip the end of the bag with scissors.

4. Create a lace pattern by making overlapping *v*'s and *e*'s in an inconsistent pattern. Practice on a plate before attempting this on the cake.

5. Using a Styrofoam cup, make a half-circle pattern around the side of the cake as shown in photo. Fill in the semicircle with the lace pattern.

6. Prepare a decorator bag with a small star tip and white frosting. Make tiny *c*'s along the edge of the semicircle. Make *w*'s on the bottom border.

7. Place fresh flowers on the top of the cake.

Monogrammed hearts adorn this appealing bridal shower cake. This cake can also be created for Valentine's Day or an anniversary.

CAKE AND FROSTING

2 (8- to 10-inch) round cakes (any flavor), baked, cooled, and refrigerated

1 batch White Wonder Cream Frosting

TOOLS AND TIPS

Cake plate	Three plastic decorator	Rose tip
Turntable	bags	Heart cookie cutter
Metal spatula	Small star tip	Scissors
Pink food color paste	Small writing tip	Long knife or dental floss

TOPPINGS

Red Hots® candy

2 Kellogg's™ Fruit Streamers™, red and pink

1. Remove the cakes from the refrigerator. Level each cake with a long knife or dental floss. Spread White Wonder Cream Frosting or other filling on one of the cakes and place the other cake on top to make a filled cake.

2. Spread White Wonder Cream Frosting over the filled cake. Smooth with a spatula.

3. Mix 1½ cups frosting with pink paste. Continue adding pink paste until you get the color you want. Prepare a decorator bag with a small star tip and pink frosting. Snip the end of the bag with scissors. Prepare a second bag using pink frosting and the writing tip.

4. Using the star tip, make *ℓ*'s and small *j*'s around the top border. Make *w*'s around the top of the cake.

5. Unroll a Fruit Streamer and carefully wrap around the bottom border. Cut the roll to fit.

6. Using a writing tip, write *love* around the bottom border of the cake.

7. With a heart cookie cutter, make two heart shapes overlapping each other.

8. Using the writing tip, make small *w*'s around the heart shapes. Write the first initials of the couple being married, one in each heart.

9. Prepare a decorator bag with a rose tip and white frosting. Snip the end of the bag with scissors. Make three white roses and two rosebuds, see page 25 for instructions. Place the roses above the hearts on the edge of the cake.

10. Decorate around the cake with Red Hots.

SWEET ROSE

This gorgeous cake is so stunning the bride-to-be will think it's her wedding cake! You can change the colors of the cake to the bride's wedding colors.

CAKE AND FROSTING

2 (8- to 10-inch) round cakes (any flavor), baked, cooled, and refrigerated
1 batch White Wonder Cream Frosting

TOOLS AND TIPS

Cake plate	Three plastic decorator	Rose tip
Turntable	bags	Leaf tip
Metal spatula	Pink food color paste	Long knife or dental floss
Chopsticks	Green food color paste	
Scissors	Small star tip	

STEP-BY-STEP

1. Remove the cakes from the refrigerator. Level each cake with a long knife or dental floss. Spread White Wonder Cream Frosting or

other filling on one of the cakes and place the other cake on top to make a filled cake.

2. Spread White Wonder Cream Frosting over the filled cake. Smooth with a spatula.

3. Mix 1 cup frosting with pink paste. Continue adding pink paste until you get the color you want. Prepare a decorator bag with the small star tip and pink frosting. Snip the end of the bag with scissors. Make long *ℓ*'s around the top of the cake. Make a large swirl of *e*'s in the center of the cake to give height to the roses.

4. Mix 1½ cups frosting with pink paste. Add some powdered sugar to the frosting to make it stiffer for making roses. Prepare a decorator bag with the rose tip and pink frosting. Snip the end of the bag with scissors. Make five roses (see page 25 for instructions), placing four on the side of the center swirl and one on the top.

5. Using the rose tip, make wide *w*'s around the top border and the bottom border.

6. Mix ¾ cups frosting with green paste. Prepare a decorator bag with the leaf tip and green frosting. Snip the end of the bag with scissors. Make small leaves around the cake.

7. Using the star tip, make one *ℓ* and one upside down *ℓ* continuously around the side of the cake.

seven

Celebration Cakes

This celebration cake can be used for a variety of events, from a good report card, promotion, or a big accomplishment to a sports victory or graduation!

CAKE AND FROSTING

1 (9 x 13-inch) rectangular cake (any flavor), baked, cooled, and refrigerated

1 batch White Wonder Cream Frosting

TOOLS AND TIPS

Cake plate	Bamboo sticks	Yellow food color paste
Turntable	Scissors	Medium star tip
Metal spatula	Plastic decorator bag	Long knife or dental floss

TOPPINGS

AirHeads® candy, variety of colors	Skittles® colored fruit-flavored candies, or	Pixy Stix®
Candy sticks	other similar candy	Mike and Ike® candies

STEP-BY-STEP

1. Remove the cake from the refrigerator. Level the cake with a long knife or dental floss.

2. Spread White Wonder Cream Frosting over the cake. Smooth with a spatula.

3. With scissors, cut the AirHeads candies into thirds lengthwise to make streamers. Carefully wrap each strip (reserving four strips) around a bamboo stick. Put the sticks on a plate and put in the freezer until firm, about 5 minutes.

4. With scissors, snip the end of one or more Pixy Stix and sprinkle over the top of the cake. Use one color or mix them up.

5. Mix white frosting with yellow paste. Continue adding yellow paste until you get the color you want. Prepare a decorator bag with a medium star tip and yellow frosting. Snip the end of the bag with scissors. Make *w*'s around the bottom border and *j*'s around the top border. Make long *c*'s on the top of the cake.

6. Once the streamers are firm, gently slide the candy off the stick and make "party sticks." Hold three streamers against a candy stick and wrap with a reserved AirHead candy strip. Repeat the process with the other candy sticks and streamers. Place the remaining streamers around the bottom of the cake.

6. Press the colorful candies and Mike and Ike candies on top of the cake and into the middle of the sides of the cake.

Make this cake for someone who deserves a soothing bubble bath. It's an adorable hot tub cake—perfect for someone retiring or who has competed a large task. Everyone will want to just dive in and enjoy the bubbles!

CAKE AND FROSTING

2 (8- to 10-inch) round cakes (any flavor), baked, cooled, and refrigerated

1 batch White Wonder Cream Frosting

> **Jill's Tip:** If serving this cake to small children, remove the gum pieces before serving to prevent choking or swallowing the gum. You can substitute the gumballs with other round candies.

TOOLS AND TIPS

Cake plate	Three plastic decorator	Scissors
Turntable	bags	Long knife or dental floss
Metal spatula	Medium star tip	
Blue food color paste	Large star tip	

TOPPINGS

Gumballs, variety of	Round sugar cookies
colors	Neapolitan wafer cookies

1. Remove the cakes from the refrigerator. Level each cake with a long knife or dental floss. Spread White Wonder Cream Frosting or other filling on one of the cakes and place the other cake on top to make a filled cake.

2. Spread White Wonder Cream Frosting over the filled cake. Smooth with a spatula.

3. Tuck sugar cookies into the bottom of the cake to make a rug.

4. Press wafer cookies on the side of the cake to create the frame of the hot tub.

5. Mix 2 cups frosting with blue paste. Continue adding blue paste until you get the color you want. Prepare a decorator bag with a large star tip and blue frosting. Snip the end of the bag with scissors. Make *e*'s around the center of the cake to make bubbling water in the tub.

6. Prepare a decorator bag with a large star tip and white frosting. Snip the end of the bag with scissors. Make *j*'s around the top of the border.

7. Place a sugar cookie in the water to make a face. Put a small amount of blue frosting in a decorator bag. Make a tiny snip at the end of the bag, then pipe hair, eyes, and mouth onto the cookie.

8. With the blue star-tip bag, make a swirl on the cookies rug.

9. Decorate the cake using gumballs.

Jill's Tip: Make the tub all one color by using vanilla or chocolate wafer cookies, or mix them at random for a colorful look.

Graduating is one of life's biggest accomplishments. From finishing kindergarten to getting a doctorate degree, every graduation is special and deserves a celebration. This cake rejoices with a diploma and a mortar cap.

CAKE AND FROSTING

2 (8- to 10-inch) round cakes (any flavor), baked, cooled, and refrigerated
1 batch White Wonder Cream Frosting

TOOLS AND TIPS

Cake plate	Three plastic decorator	Medium star tip
Turntable	bags	Small star tip
Metal spatula	Blue food color paste	Small writing tip
Scissors	Green food color paste	Long knife or dental floss

TOPPINGS

Dark chocolate squares	Red licorice strings
Oreo® cookies	Swiss Cake Rolls

1. Remove the cakes from the refrigerator. Level each cake with a long knife or dental floss. Spread White Wonder Cream Frosting or other filling on one of the cakes and place the other cake on top to make a filled cake.

2. Spread White Wonder Cream Frosting over the filled cake. Smooth with a spatula.

3. Mix 1½ cups frosting with blue paste. Continue adding blue paste until you get the color you want. Prepare a decorator bag with the medium star tip and blue frosting. Snip the end of the bag with scissors. Make *h*'s around the bottom border and *j*'s on the top border. Make long *w*'s on the top of the cake to make clouds.

4. Cut the ends of two Swiss cake rolls and stick together to make a scroll. Lay on the cake, slightly off-center. Prepare a decorator bag with the small star tip and White Wonder Cream Frosting. Snip the end with scissors. Make long lines along the side of the cake rolls. Swirl *e*'s on the ends of the cake rolls.

5. Remove the white center of an Oreo cookie and hold two chocolate cookies together with a dab of frosting that won't be seen. Place another dab of frosting on top to hold a chocolate square in place to make the mortar cap.

6. With scissors, cut licorice into 1-inch pieces to make a scroll and hat tassels. Add a dab of White Wonder Cream Frosting on the top of the cap and insert the licorice pieces. Repeat to make as many caps as you'd like.

7. Mix ½ cup frosting with green paste. Continue adding green paste until you get the color you want. Prepare a decorator bag with the small writing tip and green frosting. Snip the end of the bag with scissors. Write sentiments on the cake, such as Congratulations or Hats Off.

Blue ribbons signify doing the best! Whether it's for being first place in a competition or telling someone she's number one in your life, this ribbon cake will be the big winner!

CAKE AND FROSTING

2 (8- to 10-inch) round cakes (any flavor), baked, cooled, and refrigerated

2 batches White Wonder Cream Frosting (double recipe)

TOOLS AND TIPS

Cake plate	Two plastic decorator	Medium star tip
Turntable	bags	Small star tip
Metal spatula	Blue food color paste	Styrofoam coffee cup
Scissors	Yellow food color paste	Long knife or dental floss

TOPPINGS

Lemonhead® candies   Red licorice twists

1. Remove the cakes from the refrigerator. Level each cake with a long knife or dental floss. Spread White Wonder Cream Frosting or other filling on one of the cakes and place the other cake on top to make a filled cake.

2. Spread White Wonder Cream Frosting over the filled cake. Smooth with a spatula.

3. Using a coffee cup, make a circle print in the center of the cake.

4. Mix 1½ cups frosting with blue paste. Continue adding blue paste until you get the color you want. Prepare a decorator bag with a medium star tip and blue frosting. Snip the end of the bag with scissors. Make *w*'s continuously around the top of the cake to make a large blue ribbon. Use your circle print as your guide.

5. Make *h*'s around the bottom border and *w*'s on the side of the cake.

6. Lay four licorice twists together in your hand. With scissors, cut the licorice at an angle. Repeat for the other ribbon.

7. Insert licorice ribbons into the filling middle of the cake and let the ends of the ribbon rest on the plate.

8. Decorate around the cake with lemon drops.

9. Mix a small amount of white frosting with yellow paste. Prepare a decorator bag with a small star tip. Snip the end of the bag with scissors. Make a number one in the center of the cake.

This sunny cake will bring bright smiles to your friends and family. Select different styles of sunglasses for your party theme.

> **Jill's Tip:** Make this with lemon cake, and you'll have a wonderful summer dessert.

CAKE AND FROSTING

2 (8- to 10-inch) round cakes (any flavor), baked, cooled, and refrigerated
1 batch Lemon Wonder Cream Frosting

TOOLS AND TIPS

Cake plate	Sharp knife	Yellow food color paste
Turntable	Scissors	Medium star tip
Metal spatula	Plastic decorator bag	Long knife or dental floss

TOPPINGS

Sunglasses	Lemon-iced soft cookies	Lemon drops

STEP-BY-STEP

1. Remove the cakes from the refrigerator. Level each cake with a long knife or dental floss.

2. Spread Lemon Wonder Cream Frosting over one of the cakes. Smooth with a spatula.

3. With a sharp knife, cut the cookies into triangles. Place the cookies around the top edge of the cake.

4. With frosting, fill in the rest of the bottom layer of the cake.

5. On a separate plate, spread frosting on the second cake. Smooth with a spatula. Carefully lift and place on top of the cookies.

6. Mix the rest of the frosting with yellow paste. Continue adding yellow paste until you get the color you want. Prepare a decorator bag with a medium star tip and yellow frosting. Snip the end of the bag with scissors. Make *w*'s around the top of the cake to make the sun's face. Add lemon drops after each layer of *w*'s. Make extended *l*'s around the bottom border.

7. Place sunglasses in the middle of the cake.

This inspirational cake is for those who want to soar in life. It symbolizes the change a caterpillar must go through to become a beautiful butterfly that will fly to new heights. Use this cake to celebrate any victory, new job, new career, accomplishment, or graduation. The sky's the limit!

CAKE AND FROSTING

2 (8- to 10-inch) round cakes (any flavor), baked, cooled, and refrigerated
1 batch White Wonder Cream Frosting

TOOLS AND TIPS

Cake plate	Two plastic decorator	Medium star tip
Turntable	bags	Long knife or dental floss
Metal spatula	Blue food color paste	
Scissors	Medium writing tip	

TOPPINGS

Sour gummy worms	Gumballs	Green sour rope
Peach slices candy	Large gumballs	Pixy Stix®

1. Remove the cakes from the refrigerator. Level each cake with a long knife or dental floss. Spread White Wonder Cream Frosting or other filling on one of the cakes and place the other cake on top to make a filled cake.

2. Spread White Wonder Cream Frosting over the filled cake. Smooth with a spatula.

3. Mix 1½ cups frosting with blue paste. Continue adding blue paste until you get the color you want. Prepare a decorator bag with a writing tip and blue frosting. Snip the end of the bag with scissors. Make *l*'s around the bottom border. On the top border, write the word *fly* and three *w*'s continuously around the cake.

4. Prepare a decorator bag with a star tip and white frosting. Snip the end of the bag with scissors. In the middle of the cake, make a swirl of *o*'s like soft-serve ice cream.

5. With scissors, cut peach slices in half. Using white frosting, make a small swirl on the edge of the cake to prop up the butterfly. Place a gummy worm in the middle of the swirl and add the two peach slices on both sides to make butterfly wings. Cut two small pieces of green sour rope to make the antennas. Repeat assembly to make seven butterflies. Two of the butterflies rest in the middle of the cake.

6. Make a caterpillar by sticking one large gumball and four small gumballs into the side of the cake around the bottom edge. Make eyes by cutting a small circle of green sour rope; affix with a dot of frosting. Make antennas by cutting a short piece of sour rope. Insert into the top of the caterpillar head.

7. Decorate with gumballs and Pixy Stix.

Say "thanks" with a flower basket. The recipient will be pleasantly surprised to find it's an edible basket of flowers! This colorful cake can adorn any table for a variety of occasions.

CAKE AND FROSTING

3 (8- to 10-inch) round cakes (any flavor), baked, cooled, and refrigerated

1 batch White Wonder Cream Frosting

Cake plate	Bamboo sticks	Medium star tip
Turntable	Scissors	Long knife or dental floss
Metal spatula	Plastic decorator bag	

TOPPINGS

Fresh or silk flowers	Necco® Wafers	Pink licorice twists

STEP-BY-STEP

1. Remove the cakes from the refrigerator. Level each cake with a long knife or dental floss. Spread White Wonder Cream Frosting or other filling on two of the cakes. Carefully, stack the frosted cakes on top of each other, pressing them to fit securely. Place the third cake on top to make a tall filled cake.

2. Spread White Wonder Cream Frosting over the filled cake. Smooth with a spatula.

3. Prepare a decorator bag with a medium star tip and white frosting. Snip the end of the bag with scissors. Make *e*'s around the bottom border and *j*'s around the top border.

4. Cut four 2-inch pieces of bamboo sticks. With scissors, cut the ends of three licorice twists. Take one licorice and attach the bamboo stick piece on each end. Insert the other licorice on both sides. This is your basket handle. Measure the handle to see how it fits over the cake. Cut to the right length and insert the bamboo stick pieces. Insert the handle into the cake.

5. Press Necco Wafers into the sides of the cake.

6. Insert fresh or silk flowers into the cake top.

eight

In His Steps
Religious Cakes

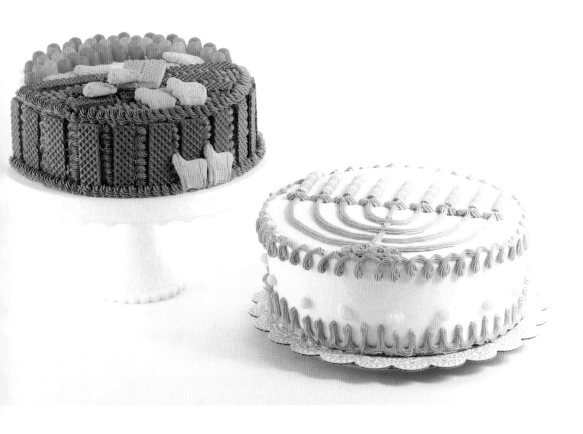

CHRISTENING GOWN

Children are God's greatest blessings, and many churches rejoice in new life with a dedication, christening, or baptismal service. Afterwards, when friends and family join together to celebrate this joyous moment, bring out this pretty cake.

CAKE AND FROSTING

1 (9 x 13-inch) rectangular cake (any flavor), baked, cooled, and refrigerated

2 batches White Wonder Cream Frosting (double recipe)

TOOLS AND TIPS

Rectangular cake plate
   or white cutting board

Turntable

Metal spatula

Scissors

Two plastic decorator
   bags

Pink or blue food color
   paste

Medium star tip

Small star tip

Rose tip

Long knife or dental floss

Pastel mint lentils or pillow mints, green and white

STEP-BY-STEP

1. Remove the cake from the refrigerator. Cut it in half and level each half with a long knife or dental floss. Spread White Wonder Cream Frosting or other filling on top of one of the halves. Place the other cake half on top.

2. Spread White Wonder Cream Frosting over the filled cake. Smooth with a spatula.

3. Prepare a decorator bag with a medium star tip and white frosting. Snip the end of the bag with scissors.

4. Make *e*'s along the bottom border. Make small *w*'s along the top border.

5. Mix 2 cups white frosting with pink or blue paste. Continue adding pink or blue paste until you get the color you want. Prepare a decorator bag with a small star tip and pink or blue frosting. Snip the end of the bag with scissors. First make the neck outline of a gown by making a half-circle of *w*'s. Make the outline of the sleeves and the drape of the gown (like a flowing, upside-down *v*). Finish with the sides of the gown. In the middle, make two bows by writing a cursive capital *j* and attaching two ribbon lines.

6. Prepaer another decorator bag with the rose tip and pink or blue frosting. Make one single rose in the middle of the gown using the rose tip. (See page 25 for instructions.) Make three roses in the front bottom border.

7. Use green pastel mint lentils to make leaves. Decorate the rest of the gown with white lentils.

> **Jill's Tip:** If your frosting is not stiff enough to make a rose, add powdered sugar and mix until smooth and stiff.

Noah's ark is one of the most beloved Bible stories. This adorable cake can be used for a variety of occasions—whenever you want a reminder of God's promise and hope.

CAKE AND FROSTING

2   (8- to 10-inch) round cakes (any flavor), baked, cooled, and refrigerated
1   batch White Wonder Cream Frosting

TOOLS AND TIPS

Cake plate	Two Plastic decorator	Small star tip
Turntable	bags	Scissors
Metal spatula	Medium star tip	Long knife or dental floss

TOPPINGS

Chocolate and vanilla	Large animal crackers	Dots® candy
sugar wafer cookies	Tub of chocolate frosting	

1. Remove the cakes from the refrigerator. Level each cake with a long knife or dental floss. Spread White Wonder Cream Frosting or other filling on one of the cakes and place the other cake on top to make a filled cake.

2. Spread White Wonder Cream Frosting over the filled cake. Smooth with a spatula.

3. Press chocolate wafer cookies around the side of the cake in a half-circle to form a boat. Leave a little space between the cookies for cutting. Place more wafer cookies across the top of the cake to fill in the boat (see photo).

4. Prepare a decorator bag with a star tip and chocolate frosting. Snip the end of the bag with scissors. Make tight w's in between the wafer cookies. Make tight c's along the top and bottom borders of the boat.

5. Press two vanilla wafer cookies on the top of the boat to make a ramp.

6. Dab some chocolate frosting on the backs of the animal crackers and place them around the boat. Put them in pairs.

7. Prepare a decorator bag with a small star tip and white frosting. Snip the end of the bag with scissors. Make w's around the top and bottom borders of the top half of the cake.

8. Make a rainbow above the boat with Dots candy pieces as shown, pressing the pieces into the frosting.

The cross is probably the most significant symbol of a Christian life. This easy-to-make cross cake surrounded by roses can be used for a baby dedication, first communion, baptism, confirmation, and on holy days or Easter Sunday.

CAKE AND FROSTING

2 (8- to 10-inch) round cakes (any flavor), baked, cooled, and refrigerated

1 batch White Wonder Cream Frosting

TOOLS AND TIPS

Cake plate	Sharp knife	Scissors
Turntable	Plastic decorator bag	Long knife or dental floss
Metal spatula	Medium star tip	

TOPPINGS

White and light green AirHeads® candy

Chocolate wafer cookies

STEP-BY-STEP

1. Remove the cakes from the refrigerator. Level each cake with a long knife or dental floss. Spread White Wonder Cream Frosting or other filling on one of the cakes and place the other cake on top to make a filled cake.

2. Spread White Wonder Cream Frosting over the filled cake. Smooth with a spatula.

3. Make eleven rosebuds by rolling AirHead candies tightly in a swirl lengthwise, keeping one end open to make the top of the rosebud. Squeeze the bottom of the rose to make the stem of the flower. Repeat the process for all the rosebuds needed. Put the rosebuds on a plate and place them in the freezer until firm and set, about 5 minutes. (See the illustrations on page 39.)

4. Prepare a decorator bag with a medium star tip and white frosting. Snip the end of the bag with scissors. Make *e*'s along the bottom border. Make small *y*'s along the top border.

5. Lay a wafer cookie in the middle of the cake. Using a sharp knife, cut another chocolate wafer cookie in half to make the sides of a cross.

6. When the rosebuds are chilled and firm, place them around the bottom of the cross and the upper corners of the cake.

7. With scissors, cut leaf shapes with light green AirHeads. Place among the roses.

Baby Jesus lying in a manger is a simple yet meaningful display for any Christmas celebration.

CAKE AND FROSTING

2   (8- to 10-inch) round cakes (any flavor), baked, cooled, and refrigerated
1   batch White Wonder Cream Frosting

TOOLS AND TIPS

Cake plate	Two plastic decorator	Waxed or parchment
Turntable	bags	paper
Metal spatula	Small star tip	Long knife or dental floss
Scissors	Madium star tip	Green food coloring paste

TOPPINGS

Ice-cream waffle bowl	Vanilla wafer	Red Hots® candy

1. Remove the cakes from the refrigerator. Level each cake with a long knife or dental floss. Spread White Wonder Cream Frosting or other filling on one of the cakes and place the other cake on top to make a filled cake.

2. Spread White Wonder Cream Frosting over the filled cake. Smooth with a spatula.

3. Prepare a decorator bag with a star tip and white frosting. Snip the end of the bag with scissors. Make n's along the bottom border. Make w's along the top border.

4. Lay a waffle bowl in the middle of the cake. Fill with white frosting. Insert a vanilla wafer (baby's head).

5. Cut a square of waxed or parchment paper. Fold it in half diagonally to make a triangle large enough to cover the waffle bowl.

6. Spread frosting evenly over the paper triangle, going over the edges. Smooth with a spatula. Once the frosting is smooth, lift up with your fingers and gently place over the waffle bowl.

7. With the star tip, make extended ℓ's along the border of the blanket. Write *j-o-y* on top of the blanket.

8. Mix the rest of the frosting with green paste. Continue adding green paste until you get the color you want. Prepare a decorator bag with a medium star tip and green frosting. Snip the end of the bag with scissors. To make holly leaves, write three w's on one side and three w's on the opposing side, connecting on the ends. Fill in the leaf with green frosting. Make holly leaves around the top and the side of the cake. Use three Red Hots for holly berries.

This beautiful Bible cake is a wonderful complement to any religious event. Change the color of the roses for the different seasons or theme of the occasion.

CAKE AND FROSTING

1 (9 x 13-inch) rectangular cake (any flavor), baked, cooled, and refrigerated

2 batches White Wonder Cream Frosting (double recipe)

TOOLS AND TIPS

Rectangular cake plate or white cutting board	Yellow food color paste	Small writing tip
	Green food color paste	Large rim cup
Turntable	Medium star tip	Scissors
Metal spatula	Small star tip	Knife
Five plastic decorator bags	Rose tip	
	Leaf tip	

STEP-BY-STEP

1. Cut an inch or more from the long side of the cake (so the shape will look more like a book), making it 9 x 12 inches. Spread White Wonder Cream Frosting over the cake. Smooth with a spatula.

2. Prepare a decorator bag with a medium star tip and white frosting. Snip the end of the bag with scissors. Make long lines along three sides of the cake to look like book pages.

3. With a large cup, make a circle pattern in the upper part of the cake.

4. Mix 2 cups frosting with yellow paste. Continue adding yellow paste until you get the color you want. Prepare a decorator bag with a small star tip and yellow frosting. Snip the end of the bag with scissors. Make *ℓ*'s around the circle pattern. Make *w*'s around the top border of the cake.

5. Prepare a decorator bag with a rose tip and yellow frosting. Snip the end of the bag with scissors. Make two yellow roses and several rosebuds (see page 26 for instructions). Place the roses in the corners of the cake and the rosebuds out from the roses along the sides of the cake.

6. Mix the rest of the frosting with green paste. Prepare a decorator bag with a leaf tip and green frosting. Snip the end of the bag with scissors. Make leaves around the roses.

7. Prepare a decorator bag with a writing tip and a small amount of green frosting. Snip the end of the bag with scissors. Write *Holy Bible* in the center of circle.

Hanukkah is a sacred time for Jewish people, celebrating their miraculous survival through millennia of hardship. This cake features the Hanukkah candelabra, an enduring symbol of the eight days of Hanukkah.

CAKE AND FROSTING

2 (8- to 10-inch) round cakes (any flavor), baked, cooled, and refrigerated

1 batch White Wonder Cream Frosting

TOOLS AND TIPS

Cake plate	Blue food color paste	Ruler
Turntable	Small star tip	Long knife or dental floss
Metal spatula	Sharp knife	
Plastic decorator bag	Scissors	

TOPPINGS

Rolled wafer cookies	Lemonhead® candy

STEP-BY-STEP

1. Remove the cakes from the refrigerator. Level each cake with a long knife or dental floss. Spread White Wonder Cream Frosting or

other filling on one of the cakes and place the other cake on top to make a filled cake.

2. Spread White Wonder Cream Frosting over a cooled, level, and filled cake. Smooth with a spatula.

3. Mix the rest of the frosting with blue paste. Continue adding blue paste until you get the color you want. Prepare a decorator bag with a star tip and blue frosting. Snip the end of the bag with scissors. Make l's along the bottom border. Make j's along the top border.

4. Using a ruler, make nine equal marks along the middle of the cake. Place a dot of blue frosting to mark each spot. Connect the two outer marks (the first and ninth) by forming a large u. Continue making three more concentric w's. For the middle, make a line connecting down the menorah. Make c's for the menorah bottom. For the top of the candleholders, make little j's.

5. With a sharp knife, cut rolled cookies in equal lengths. Place on top of the candleholders.

6. Place a lemon candy on top of each cookie candle and around the side of the cake.

STAR OF DAVID

The Jewish star is a symbol of the ancient king David and has come to represent both Judaism and the modern state of Israel.

CAKE AND FROSTING

2 (8- to 10-inch) round cakes (any flavor), baked, cooled, and refrigerated

1 batch White Wonder Cream Frosting

TOOLS AND TIPS

Cake plate	Small star tip	Scissors
Turntable	Medium star tip	Ruler
Metal spatula	Medium writing tip	Long knife or dental floss
Three plastic decorator bags	Blue food color paste	
	Geen food color paste	

TOPPINGS

Yellow and dark purple Skittles® colored fruit flavored candies, or other similar candy

STEP-BY-STEP

1. Remove the cakes from the refrigerator. Level each cake with a long knife or dental floss. Spread White Wonder Cream Frosting or

other filling on one of the cakes and place the other cake on top to make a filled cake.

2. Spread White Wonder Cream Frosting over the filled cake. Smooth with a spatula.

3. With a ruler, make two triangles overlapping each other to make the star. Use the ruler to score three six-inch lines to make one triangle. Score another triangle upside down over the first triangle.

4. Mix 1½ cups frosting with blue paste. Continue adding blue paste until you get the color you want. Prepare a decorator bag with a medium star tip and blue frosting. Snip the end of the bag with scissors. Make tiny *w*'s along the star pattern. Make *s*'s along the bottom border.

5. Prepare a decorator bag with a small star tip and white frosting. Snip the end of the bag with scissors. Make *y*'s along the top border.

6. Mix ½ cups frosting with green paste. Continue adding green paste until you get the color you want. Prepare a decorator bag with a writing tip and green frosting. Snip the end of the bag with scissors. Make olive branches by drawing two-inch swerving lines and adding small *l*'s for the leaves. Decorate with yellow and purple candies.

Dessert on a Dime
Fancy Cakes

This exquisite looking cake takes just minutes to decorate. You can write anything you desire across the top to complement the special occasion. When you cut the cake, everyone gets a few cookies to enjoy as well.

CAKE AND FROSTING

2 (8- to 10-inch) round cakes (any flavor), baked, cooled, and refrigerated
1 batch White Wonder Cream Frosting

TOOLS AND TIPS

Cake plate

Turntable

Metal spatula

Scissors

Two plastic decorator
   bags

Medium star tip

Small writing tip

Long knife or dental floss

Tape

TOPPINGS

Andes® mint chocolates

Mini chocolate bar

Rolled wafer cookies
   (about 50)

One-inch ribbon (1 yard),
   beige

1. Remove the cakes from the refrigerator. Level each cake with a long knife or dental floss. Spread White Wonder Cream Frosting or other filling on one of the cakes and place the other cake on top to make a filled cake.

2. Spread White Wonder Cream Frosting over the filled cake. Smooth with a spatula.

3. Press rolled cookies around the side of the cake vertically.

4. Wrap a ribbon around the cookies. With the scissors, cut the ribbon when both ends meet. Secure the ribbon with tape or dab frosting on both ends of the ribbon to act as glue.

5. Prepare a decorator bag with a medium star tip and white frosting. Snip the end of the bag with scissors. Make *x*'s along the top border. Make *o*'s in the center ring of the cake. Make a swirl in the middle of the cake.

6. Lay the chocolate pieces on a plate flat side up. Prepare a decorator bag with a writing tip and white frosting. Snip the end of the bag with scissors. Write *x*'s and *o*'s (or other letters depending on your sentiment) on the mint chocolate pieces and *love* (or other sentiment) on the longer chocolate piece.

7. Place small chocolate pieces inside the *o* on top of the cake. Place the *love* (or other sentiment) piece in the middle.

This cherry-topped cake looks like a million bucks and is a satisfying end to an appetizing dinner.

CAKE AND FROSTING

2 (8- to 10-inch) round cakes (any flavor), baked, cooled, and refrigerated

1 batch Chocolate Wonder Cream Frosting

TOOLS AND TIPS

Cake plate	Plastic decorator bag	Scissors
Turntable	Medium star tip	Long knife or dental floss
Metal spatula	Scissors	Vegetable peeler

TOPPINGS

Cherry topping

White chocolate balls

White chocolate bar

STEP-BY-STEP

1. Remove the cakes from the refrigerator. Level each cake with a long knife or dental floss. Spread Chocolate Wonder Cream Frosting or other filling on one of the cakes and place the other cake on top to make a filled cake.

2. Spread Chocolate Wonder Cream Frosting over the filled cake. Smooth with a spatula.

3. Prepare a decorator bag with the medium star tip and Chocolate Wonder Cream Frosting. Snip the end of the bag with scissors. Write *o*'s around the bottom border. Make *o*'s along the top border. Make small *o*'s inside the edge of the border. Make a swirl of frosting in the middle of the cake.

4. Spoon cherry topping onto the cake top center.

5. Place white chocolate balls around the cake as shown in the photo.

6. Shave a white chocolate bar with a vegetable peeler, spreading the white shavings over the cherries.

CARROTS GALORE

Carrot cake is a favorite cake for many people. It seems the autumn months wouldn't be the same without a nutty carrot cake and a warm cup of cocoa.

CAKE AND FROSTING

2 (8- to 10-inch) round carrot spice cakes, baked, cooled, and refrigerated

1 batch White Wonder Cream Frosting

2 (16 oz.) tubs cream cheese frosting

TOOLS AND TIPS

Cake plate	Plastic decorator bag	Long knife or dental floss
Turntable	Medium star tip	
Metal spatula	Scissors	

TOPPINGS

Orange and green fruit chews

Chopped walnut pieces

STEP-BY-STEP

1. Remove the cakes from the refrigerator. Level each cake with a long knife or dental floss. Spread White Wonder Cream Frosting frosting or other filling on one of the cakes and place the other cake on top to make a filled cake.

2. Spread cream cheese frosting over the filled cake. Smooth with a spatula.

3. With your hand, carefully press walnuts onto the side of a cake, about one-third up from the bottom. It will form an irregular border.

4. Make candy carrots by pinching one end of the orange fruit chews. Place the carrots around the top of the cake.

5. Make leaves by cutting green fruit chews in half and making small snips. Place behind each carrot.

7. Prepare a decorator bag with a star tip and white frosting. Snip the end of the bag with scissors. Make *y*'s around the top border. Make a swirl in the middle of the cake. Sprinkle with walnut pieces.

This cake would cost a pretty penny at a bakery, but you can make it at home for less than ten dollars—and please all the coffee lovers you know!

CAKE AND FROSTING

2 (8- to 10-inch) round cakes (any flavor), baked, cooled, and refrigerated

1 batch Mocha Wonder Cream Frosting

1 batch Chocolate Wonder Cream Frosting

TOOLS AND TIPS

Cake plate	Plastic decorator bag	Long knife or dental floss
Turntable	Medium star tip	
Metal spatula	Scissors	

TOPPINGS

Chocolate espresso beans

Rolled wafer cookies

1. Remove the cakes from the refrigerator. Level each cake with a long knife or dental floss. Spread Chocolate Wonder Cream Frosting or other filling on one of the cakes and place the other cake on top to make a filled cake.

2. Spread Chocolate Wonder Cream Frosting over the filled cake. Smooth with a spatula.

3. Prepare a decorator bag with the medium star tip and Mocha Wonder Cream. Snip the end of the bag with scissors. Make *l*'s around the bottom border.

4. Make a simple basket weave by first making large *W*'s around the top edge of the cake. Make lines from one tip of a *W* to the other *W*. Next, make lines from the center of one *W* to another *W*, crossing over the line of the first *W*'s. Alternate until all the *W*'s are filled in.

5. Make *y*'s around the top border.

6. Make *l*'s in a circle in the middle of the cake. It will look like a flower.

7. Decorate with espresso beans and rolled cookies as shown in photo.

ten

Love Is in the Air! Wedding Cakes

Wedding cakes are a little more complicated than other cakes. They tend to be larger and have to be moved to a different location for the reception.

Large-sized pans—such as the ones you'll need to make tiered cakes—can be found in the cake decorating aisle in discount or craft stores. If you want to save money, see if a friend will let you borrow her set.

A nice touch to these wedding cakes is fresh flowers. Be sure to put your flowers on the cake after you have set it up where it will be served. Fresh flowers may only look pretty for a while without water; however, you can purchase flower vials at a local florist and insert each stem into a little vial of water to keep them fresh when transporting them.

When moving your cake to another location, be sure to travel carefully. Lay your cakes on a flat surface (a trunk or hatch area) and lay a towel down so they will not slide when traveling. Bring your supplies (decorator bags, tips, scissors, towel, and flowers) with you so you are ready to set up the cake when you arrive.

Bursting with summer love, this basket-weave-and-country-flower wedding cake will be a delight at any outdoor wedding. To hold the top tier, I've used three inexpensive bud vases. Everyone will fall in love with this sun-kissed beauty.

CAKE AND FROSTING

2 (8-inch) round cakes (any flavor), baked, cooled, and refrigerated

2 (12-inch) round cakes (any flavor), baked, cooled, and refrigerated

3 batches White Wonder Cream Frosting (triple recipe)

TOOLS AND TIPS

8-inch cake board	Plastic decorator bag	Apple corer or dull knife
14-inch cake plate	Small star tip	Three bud vases
Turntable	Scissors	
Metal spatula	Long knife or dental floss	

Fresh flowers

STEP-BY-STEP

1. Remove the cakes from the refrigerator. Level each cake with a long knife or dental floss. Place one 8-inch cake on the 8-inch cake board. Spread White Wonder Cream Frosting or other filling on the 8-inch cake on the board and place the other 8-inch cake on top to make a filled cake. Repeat the process with the 12-inch cakes to make a 12-inch filled cake, using the 14-inch cake plate.

2. Spread White Wonder Cream Frosting over both filled cakes. Smooth with a spatula.

3. Prepare a decorator bag with the small star tip and White Wonder Cream Frosting. Snip the end of the bag with scissors.

4. Create a basket-weave pattern on the bottom border of both the 8-inch and 12-inch cakes. Make large *w*'s around the bottom borders. Make three rows of short horizontal lines that cross the vertical lines of the *w*'s, alternating as you go.

5. Make *y*'s on the top borders of both cakes.

6. Make large horizontal *s*'s around the sides of both cakes. Add small *c*'s to the middle of the *s*'s.

7. On the 12-inch cake, the bottom tier, use an apple corer or a dull knife to hollow out three small holes to hold the bud vases. Make the holes in the middle of the cake to form a triangle. Make sure the vases will be close enough together to hold the top tier.

8. Turn the bud vases upside down and slowly insert them into the cake. Continue pressing until each vase hits the cake plate.

9. Carefully place the 8-inch cake, the top tier, on top of the vases.

10. Decorate the cake with fresh flowers. Cut the stems as necessary. Arrange the flowers so they face out.

Red roses symbolize love—so what better way to celebrate a wedding or anniversary than with this gorgeous cake. Change the color of the roses and you'll have a different look with the same elegance.

CAKE AND FROSTING

2 (8-inch) round cakes (any flavor), baked, cooled, and refrigerated

2 (12-inch) round cakes (any flavor), baked, cooled, and refrigerated

3 batches White Wonder Cream Frosting (triple recipe)

TOOLS AND TIPS

8-inch cake board	Plastic decorator bag	Sharp knife
14-inch cake plate	Small star tip	Large drinking cup
Turntable	Scissors	Long knife or dental floss
Metal spatula	Chopstick or wood dowel	

TOPPINGS

Fresh roses

STEP-BY-STEP

1. Remove the cakes from the refrigerator. Level each cake with a long knife or dental floss. Place one of the 8-inch cakes on the 8-inch cake board. Spread White Wonder Cream Frosting or other filling on the 8-inch cake on the board and place the other 8-inch cake on top to make a filled cake. Repeat the process with the 12-inch cakes to make a 12-inch filled cake, using the 14-inch cake plate.

2. Spread White Wonder Cream Frosting over both filled cakes. Smooth with a spatula.

3. Prepare a decorator bag with the small star tip and White Wonder Cream Frosting. Snip the end of the bag with scissors.

4. Make *l*'s around the bottom border.

5. Using a large drinking cup, mark a half-circle print around the side of the cake. This will be your guide to creating the draped rope look. With the decorator bag, make tiny *l*'s along the half-circle imprint.

6. Make a single upside down *l* in between each draped "rope."

7. Make small *w*'s around the top border.

8. Measure and cut four chopsticks to ⅛ to ¼ inch above the height of the cake. Make four sticks per tier. With a sharp knife, cut each stick halfway through. Snap the stick in half. Follow the instructions for stacking a tiered cake on page 13. Insert the sticks into the cake and stack the top tier on top of the bottom tier.

9. Place roses around and on top of the cake.

Where there's a wedding there's a celebration. This unique, flowing three-tiered cake using margarita glasses for columns will be a great conversation piece at the cake table.

CAKE AND FROSTING

2 (8-inch) round cakes (any flavor), baked, cooled, and refrigerated
2 (10-inch) round cakes (any flavor), baked, cooled, and refrigerated
2 (14-inch) round cakes (any flavor), baked, cooled, and refrigerated
5 batches White Wonder Cream Frosting (five recipes)

TOOLS AND TIPS

8-inch cake board	Plastic decorator bag	3 plastic wide-rimmed
10-inch cake board	Small star tip	margarita glasses
16-inch white cake plate	Scissors	(white-frosted is best)
Turntable	Hot glue gun or	Long knife or dental floss
Metal spatula	Permabond glue	

Jill's Tip: Don't have all these cake pans? You may be able to purchase undecorated cakes in various sizes from your local grocer's bakery then decorate them yourself.

TOPPINGS

Fresh flowers

STEP-BY-STEP

1. Remove the cakes from the refrigerator. Level each cake with a long knife or dental floss. Place one of the 8-inch cakes on the 8-inch cake board. Spread White Wonder Cream Frosting frosting or other filling on the 8-inch cake on the board and place the other 8-inch cake on top to make a filled cake. Repeat the process with the 10-inch cakes on the 10-inch cake board to make a 10-inch filled cake and the 14-inch cakes on the 16-inch cake board to make a 14-inch filled cake.

2. Spread White Wonder Cream Frosting over each filled cake. Smooth with a spatula.

3. Prepare a decorator bag with the small star tip and White Wonder Cream Frosting. Snip the end of the bag with scissors.

4. Make *C*'s around the bottom border of each cake and *l*'s around the top borders.

5. On sides of each cake, make two rows of uppercase cursive *J*'s followed by three small dots. Stagger the *J*'s and dots so they never line up.

6. Hot glue the bottoms of the two margarita glasses together.

7. This tiered cake features separate, not stacked, tiers; place the smallest cake on the margarita glasses that are glued together. Place the 10-inch cake on a margarita glass. Place the 14-inch cake to the side of other tiers.

8. Arrange flowers on the cake.

Simple, delicate elegance is the theme of this cake. I made this cake for a fiftieth wedding anniversary. The couple never had a wedding cake, and this was the one they'd always dreamed of!

CAKE AND FROSTING

2 (8-inch) round cakes (any flavor), baked, cooled, and refrigerated

2 (12-inch) round cakes (any flavor), baked, cooled, and refrigerated

3 batches White Wonder Cream Frosting (triple recipe)

TOOLS AND TIPS

8-inch cake board	Small star tip	Four columns and 9-inch
14-inch white cake plate	Small writing tip	cake plate (purchase
Turntable	Scissors	in the cake aisle at a
Metal spatula	Styrofoam coffee cup	discount or craft store)
Plastic decorator bag	Long knife or dental floss	

TOPPINGS

Pink roses

STEP-BY-STEP

1. Remove the cakes from the refrigerator. Level each cake with a long knife or dental floss. Place one 8-inch cake on the 8-inch cake board. Spread White Wonder Cream Frosting or other filling on the 8-inch cake on the board and place the other 8-inch cake on top to make a filled cake. Repeat the process with the 12-inch cakes to make a 12-inch filled cake. Place the 12-inch cake on the white cake plate.

2. Spread White Wonder Cream Frosting over the filled cakes. Smooth with a spatula.

3. With a Styrofoam cup, make half-circle imprints for a drape around the side of the 8-inch cake. Make half-circle imprints around the top edge of the 12-inch cake.

4. In a small bowl, thin some white frosting with a few drops of warm water. Prepare a decorator bag with a writing tip and thinned frosting. Create a lace pattern by making overlapping *s*'s and *e*'s in an inconsistent pattern. (Practice on a plate before attempting this on the cake. Refer to photo on page 105.)

5. Make extended *e*'s along the drape lines. Make single *j*'s around the side of the cake.

6. Make tight *c*'s along the bottom border of the 8-inch cake. Make large upside down *w*'s about every 2½ inches around the bottom border. Make extended *e*'s—alternating right side up and then upside down—to connect the *w*'s.

7. For the bottom tier, attach the columns to the 9-inch cake plate that came with them. Insert the columns into the top of the 12-inch cake. Continue pressing until they hit the cake plate.

8. Place the 8-inch cake on top of the columns. If you need to drive to the reception location, travel with tiers separate and not assembled.

9. Decorate with roses.

Every bride is beautiful on her wedding day—and the simple elegance of this cake will only complement her wondrous day. The pearl detail makes this cake stunning.

CAKE AND FROSTING

2 (8-inch) round cakes (any flavor), baked, cooled, and refrigerated

2 (10-inch) round cakes (any flavor), baked, cooled, and refrigerated

2 (12-inch) round cakes (any flavor), baked, cooled, and refrigerated

5 batches White Wonder Cream Frosting (five recipes)

TOOLS AND TIPS

8-inch cake board	Plastic decorator bag	Chopsticks or
10-inch cake board	Small star tip	wooden dowels
14-inch white cake plate	Small writing tip	Long knife or dental floss
Turntable	Scissors	
Metal spatula	Sharp knife	

Fresh roses

Plastic pearl strand (2 yards purchased at a discount or craft store)

STEP-BY-STEP

1. Remove the cakes from the refrigerator. Level each cake with a long knife or dental floss. Place one 8-inch cake on the 8-inch cake board. Spread White Wonder Cream Frosting or other filling on the 8-inch cake on the board and place the other 8-inch cake on top to make a filled cake. Repeat the process with the 10-inch cakes on the 10-inch cake board to make a 10-inch filled cake. Repeat the process with the 12-inch cakes on the 14-inch cake plate to make a 12-inch filled cake.

2. Spread White Wonder Cream Frosting over each filled cakes. Smooth with a spatula.

3. Prepare a decorator bag with a star tip and white frosting. Snip the end of the bag with scissors. Make *j*'s around the top border of each cake layer. (If you are transporting the cake to a reception location, wait until you have have reached the location to stack the tiers and make *j*'s around the top border.)

4. Make *e*'s or *w*'s on the bottom borders of each cake layer.

5. On the side of each cake layer, make single *v*'s. Make three dots around the side of each cake around the *v*'s.

6. Measure and cut four chopsticks to ⅛ to ¼ inch above the height of the cake. Mark four sticks per tier. With a sharp knife, cut the stick halfway through. Snap the stick in half. (Follow the instructions for stacking a tiered cake on page 13.) Insert the sticks into the cake and stack the 10-inch tier on top of the bottom tier and the 8-inch tier on top of the 10-inch tier.

7. Carefully place a pearl strand around the top and middle cake after you have stacked the cakes.

8. Add the fresh roses on the top of the cake and around the edge of the cake plate.

Jill's Tip: You can always substitute frosting roses for fresh flowers. Refer to Chapter Three for instructions.

SWEET WHITE ROSE

The top tier of this pretty cake is sitting on a large vase filled with clear marbles. However, you can fill the vase with colored marbles, flowers, or candy. Guests will think you spent hours on these AirHeads rosebuds!

CAKE AND FROSTING

2 (8-inch) round cakes (any flavor), baked, cooled, and refrigerated

2 (12-inch) round cakes (any flavor), baked, cooled, and refrigerated

3 batches White Wonder Cream Frosting (triple recipe)

TOOLS AND TIPS

8-inch cake board	Two plastic decorator	Medium writing tip
14-inch white cake plate	bags	Scissors
Turntable	Green food color paste	Long knife or dental floss
Metal spatula	Small star tip	

TOPPINGS

White and light green	Clear marbles to fill the	Large vase
AirHeads® candy	vase completely	

1. Remove the cakes from the refrigerator. Level each cake with a long knife or dental floss. Place one 8-inch cake on the 8-inch cake board. Spread White Wonder Cream Frosting or other filling on the 8-inch cake on the board and place the other 8-inch cake on top to make a filled cake. Repeat the process with the 12-inch cakes to make a 12-inch filled cake, using the 14-inch cake plate.

2. Spread White Wonder Cream Frosting over each filled cake. Smooth with a spatula.

3. Make eight rosebuds by rolling the white AirHead candies tightly in a swirl lengthwise, keeping one end open to make the top of the rosebud. (See the photos on page 39.) Squeeze the bottom of the rose to make the stem of the flower. Repeat the process for all eight rosebuds. Put the rosebuds on a plate and place them in the freezer until firm and set, about 5 minutes.

4. Prepare a decorator bag with a star tip and white frosting. Snip the end of the bag with scissors. Make $\mathcal{C}$'s around the bottom tier. Make j's and ℓ's continually around the top border.

5. Mix 1 cup frosting with green paste. Continue adding green paste until you get the color you want. Prepare a decorator bag with a writing tip and green frosting. Snip the end of the bag with scissors. Make single capital $\mathcal{V}$'s around the tops and sides of the cakes.

6. Arrange the chilled white rosebuds in the center of the cakes.

7. Flatten out the green AirHead candies. With scissors, cut small leaf shapes. Carefully place the leaves around the roses.

8. Fill the vase with marbles. Place the top tier on top of the prepared vase.

Glossary

Beat: Mix the ingredients vigorously with an electric or hand mixer.

Border: Frosting design on the edge of a cake, either on the top of the cake or the bottom edge of the cake.

Cake board: Cardboard shape to hold a cake. Cake boards are used in place of cake plates or when creating a tiered cake.

Cake plate: Flat plate large enough to hold the entire cake.

Cool: Bringing a baked item to room temperature.

Decorator bag: A plastic bag that holds a decorating tip and frosting to pipe designs onto a cake.

Decorating tip: Metal or plastic attachments that make designs when frosting is funneled through them.

Filling: Substance put between layers of a cake. Most fillings consist of frosting, fruit toppings, fresh fruit, pudding, or mousse toppings.

Food color paste: Edible coloring added to frosting to create vibrant colors used for decorating cakes.

Frost: Process of smoothing frosting evenly over a cake surface.

Frosting: Sweet topping on a cake, usually consisting of powdered sugar and shortening or butter.

Level: Cake that is the same height all around and is horizontal to the cake plate.

Mix: Combine ingredients to evenly distribute through the mixture.

Smooth: Evenly spread frosting on a cake.

Snip: Cut off a small piece of a plastic decorator bag with scissors.

Toppings: Items placed on or around a cake. Toppings can include candies, fresh or silk flowers, or decorative items.

Tiers: Two or more decorated cakes that are stacked or separated by columns. Most wedding cakes are tiered cakes.

Turntable: Spinning plate that enables a cake to turn easily while being decorated.

AirHeads®

Atomic Fireball®

Chiclets Fruit Flavor Gum®

Creme Wafers®

Dum Dum Pops®

Hostess Cup Cakes®

Fruit Roll-Ups®

Lemonhead Candies®

Mike & Ike Candies®

Necco Candy Wafers®

Sweethearts®

Peeps Bunnies®

Red Hots®

Index